TALES ALONG THE GRAND STRAND

of South Carolina

Tales along the Grand Strand
of South Carolina

Blanche W. Floyd

Winston-Salem, North Carolina

Library of Congress Catalog Card Number 96-84627

ISBN 1-878177-08-7

Bandit Books, Inc.
P.O. Box 11721
Winston-Salem, NC 27116-1721
(910) 785-7417

Excerpt on page 7 from "Indian Children" by Annette Wynne

Text photos are courtesy of J. K. Floyd unless otherwise noted

Cover photo by Will & Deni McIntyre

Cover design by Monica Cox

For Mary
who shared a love
of the sand and sea
and tales of the
Grand Strand

Table of Contents

Acknowledgments

My special heartfelt thanks go to everyone who helped make this venture a reality. Friends offered encouragement and important suggestions. Many people shared their memories, keepsakes, and family pictures. Expert editorial comments from my publisher kept me pretty much on line.

No one was more willing to help than the staff of Chapin Memorial Library in Myrtle Beach. They, too, were interested in our stories and their assistance was invaluable.

My sincere appreciation goes to my family members, who offered support and encouragement, especially my husband, J. K. He was my driver, my trusted photographer, and my tireless proof-reader. I accused him of working overtime to find my mistakes. He helped in countless ways including making copies, numbering pages, and mailing all the materials that went into the making of this book.

Ed. Note: Many thanks go to Stewart Pabst of the Horry County Museum for help in obtaining photos.

Introduction

The matchless beauty of the Grand Strand has attracted visitors literally for centuries. In some places the beach stretches more than five hundred feet wide at low tide; from the ever churning, foaming water to the sea oats waving proudly on the high sand dunes. This marvelous sight contrasts with the rocky shores of New England or the monolith rocks along the shoals and bays of Oregon and the west coast.

The Grand Strand includes all beaches and communities from the North Carolina line to Georgetown, a distance of sixty miles. Myrtle Beach lies near the center of this stretch. The word "strand" is of Anglo-Saxon origin, brought to the New World by English colonists. A synonym of strand is "shore," meaning "water's edge." To draw tourists to the growing resort, publicists in the 1920s coined the phrase, "Myrtle Beach, America's Finest Strand." After the settling and naming of other beaches, "Grand Strand" became a more inclusive name, thus preserving a term rooted in Teutonic and English heritage. The use of strand is almost unique to the South Carolina coast, since other resorts use the terms beach, shore, coast, or seaside.

Whatever the reason for coming, visitors and residents have always left their marks on the area. Some left legends or legacies, memories that have a way of vanishing unless they are written and preserved. The Grand Strand is alive with tales of bloodthirsty pirates, lurking U-boats, apparitions, natural disasters, and a unique history. This book contains some of those stories.

Enjoy them!

Spanish Travelers along the Grand Strand in 1526

The first Europeans came to the Carolina coast in 1526, attempting to establish a tenuous hold on the North American continent. Following the voyages of Columbus, Spain had developed a lucrative trade with the Caribbean Islands and the coast of Central America and Mexico. Rich cargoes of gold, silver, and raw materials came across the Atlantic in tiny, frail, sailing ships. Spaniards talked about the possibility of finding an entire continent of unknown treasures north of the islands.

In 1520 a wealthy planter on Hispaniola (Santa Domingo) named Lucas Vasquez de Ayllon received permission to establish a Spanish colony north of Florida. He sent his captain, Francisco Gordillo, to explore and choose an appropriate site. A storm drove Gordillo's ship into a river and bay in the land the Indians called *Chicora*. We know it as Winyah Bay at Georgetown, South Carolina.

As the sailing vessels approached, the Indians watched in terror, thinking they saw great white birds afloat in the bay. Gordillo landed and made friends with the Indians, then took 150 of them prisoner to sell as slaves in the islands. Thus began the long record of enslavement and brutality to the Native Americans.

De Ayllon accepted Gordillo's recommendation of Winyah Bay. The expedition was organized and set out from Hispaniola in mid-July, 1526, already past the time for planting the food crops the colonists would need. There were five ships, laden with supplies and over five hundred colonists, with De Ayllon sailing aboard the flagship. The fleet first sailed into the Cape Fear River harbor by mistake. One ship ran aground in the river and was lost, along with valuable supplies. The hardy colonists cut trees and hurriedly built a small boat with one sail to accompany the other ships.

De Ayllon decided to both sail and walk down the coast to Winyah. The men and horses traveled along the strand, with the women and children on board the ships. These Spanish men, Friars, soldiers, and adventurers, were the first Europeans to set foot on the South Carolina coast.

All along the way, the coastal Indians came to gape in wonder at the strange men and animals. They had never seen horses or guns or armor. The Spaniards took what they wanted from the Indians, treated them harshly, and moved on. Some of the Indians contracted diseases that proved fatal.

Somewhere on the north shore of Winyah Bay the women and children came ashore to join the men. Full of hopes and dreams, they began the hard task of building and establishing a colony for Spain and the Catholic Church. De Ayllon called his settlement *San Miguel de Gualdape.* The name honored Saint Michael and used the Indian word *Gualdape,* which meant "mouth of the ancient rivers." De Ayllon hoped his village would become a great city, the capital of New Spain in America.

At first the Spanish settlement seemed to have every chance of success: plentiful fish and game, fresh water, trees to cut for cabins and firewood, and family groups to set up a stable colony. They planned on using the Indians for finding additional food, and to provide slave labor for building cabins, clearing fields, and planting. Of course the Spaniards also expected them to deliver gold and silver.

The Indians, having no desire to be enslaved, refused to help. When Spanish soldiers tried to capture Indian workers, they couldn't find them. The Indians simply disappeared into the thick pine forests or river swamps.

The Spaniards found no trace of gold or silver.

In the hot, humid weather of August and September, the killing "swamp fevers" began. Malaria and yellow fever, spread by mosquitoes, struck down the Spaniards who had no immunity and no cure. Almost every family dug graves for their loved ones, while their hatred of this strange land grew. De Ayllon died in mid-October, and the survivors refused to work for the new leader.

An unusually early freeze killed the mosquitoes and stopped the fevers, yet the now frail and sickly colonists continued to die of starvation and diseases. Instead of finding wealth and power, the colony faced extinction. Only 150 out of the original 500 colonists were left.

Less than six months after their arrival, the survivors boarded the ships to return to Hispaniola. A winter gale struck, sinking one ship and bringing on more freezing temperatures.

The colonists who reached Hispaniola told their stories of suffering, and discouraged other Spanish attempts at settling north of Florida.

The site of the Winyah colony has not been definitely located. Armordale, a former plantation on Waccamaw Neck, got its name from pieces of metal armor and trappings found by hunters and explorers. Many locations have been carefully examined, but in the two hundred years before English settlers established Georgetown, signs of San Miguel were well hidden by native trees and bushes.

The dream of a great city has remained buried.

This shell midden near Waties Island, left by seafood loving
Indians, dates back more than 2,000 years. Other middens
have been radiocarbon dated to about 3,300 years ago.
Courtesy of the Horry County Museum

2

Indian Heritage along the Coast

Where we walk to school each day,
Indian children used to play.

Annette Wynne

Excavations along the Grand Strand always turn up Indian artifacts, a reminder of our coastal and national heritage. Indians were the first residents and the first tourists. Different tribes journeyed to the coast to enjoy all kinds of seafood. Archaeological digs have uncovered mounds of shells and pottery, remains of ancient fires, and evidence of village sites and burial grounds.

The King's Highway was first a meandering Indian path, used for centuries in seasonal migrations. Other paths from upstate North Carolina and all over South Carolina followed the rivers to the coast.

Tribes of the Siouan Nation had migrated from the Great Plains over hundreds of years to find places where food was plentiful and the climate favorable. Some of them found it in South Carolina's coastal regions.

The Indians lived in small villages or camps in the thick forests just back of the shore, or along creeks flowing into the Waccamaw River. Each village had a "great house" built of upright pine logs, thatched with grasses and chinked with mud.

Scientists have found the outlines of partially cleared fields where grain and vegetables grew. Some Indians made a palatable flour from acorns for porridge or bread. Sometimes they found patches of wild rice. The countryside was full of game, while the creeks and rivers teemed with fish, handy for spearing. Along the coastal inlets the Indians found shrimp, crabs, oysters, and fish.

For clothing the Indians used moss and woven straw matting in summer, and animal skins in winter. Deer were so plentiful that the first trade with the English in the early 1700s was mainly in deer skins. In England deerskin caps became popular. They were sometimes called "Carolina caps."

Some Indians were victims of diseases like smallpox and tuberculosis, acquired from contact with earlier visitors, mainly the Spanish in 1526. Measles was also a killer disease for the children.

Indian Medicine Men made wild cherry syrup for coughs, salves of pine resin and grease for skin lesions, and herbs and cooling mud packs for high fevers. But these remedies offered little defense against deadly epidemics that decimated the tribes.

Constant petty wars accounted for the deaths of many braves. Without their strong young warriors, a small tribe could easily be conquered or absorbed into a surviving tribe.

This civilization went on without much change, generation after generation. As a nomadic people, the Indians' habit was to settle for a time, then move on, following the hunt or looking for another favorable place to settle.

This simple way of life disappeared with the coming of Europeans.

The entire coastal region, from the Savannah River to the Cape Fear River in North Carolina, was called *Chicora*. The name has evolved from other spellings: *Chiquola and Shakoree*. Its meaning, "dwelling at a distance," refers to the extent of the land. The main town for many tribes was located on the Santee River.

Dozens of Grand Strand geographical names date back to the

Indians. The most familiar one today is Waccamaw, the name given to the winding river flowing through the eastern half of Horry County. The name is made up of two Indian words: *Wanki,* meaning "going," and *Ma,* meaning "coming," and refers to the tidal nature of the river itself. The Waccamaw Tribe, the largest and strongest of the small tribes, lived peacefully along the river before the settlers came.

The Pee Dee River was named for the Pee Dee Tribe, although another theory credits Patrick Daly, an explorer who cut his initials on a tree by the river.

Socastee is similar to *Sokkosete,* which means "to wash." Another similar name is *Sokhee,* meaning "convulsive or fitty." The Socastees were a minor tribe, but the name is well-known today. The Intracoastal Waterway follows Socastee Swamp for several miles.

Wampee, a community inland from Ocean Drive, may have been named after the word for tubers of the water lily plant, an Indian food.

The Lumber River, which flows into the Pee Dee, takes its name from the Lumbee Indians, who still live in that part of North Carolina.

The original plantation of Wachesaw at Murrells Inlet rested almost entirely on an old Indian burial ground. *Wachesaw* means "place of the great weeping," and "happy hunting ground."

Hobcaw, an Indian word meaning "between the waters," aptly describes the Waccamaw Neck location of Hobcaw Barony.

Black River, which flows into Winyah Bay, was known at one time as Weenau, or Weeneau River. This became the name of the wide beautiful bay, fronting the historic old town of Georgetown.

The spelling of all Indian names suffered in their translation. However, English settlers and record keepers made a stab at phonetic spelling, giving us the pleasant names familiar to us today.

The Horry County Museum in Conway has on display artifacts,

models, and pictures of Indian cultures, reminders of part of America's unique heritage.

3

Piracy

Scourge of the 1700s

On a hazy day have you glimpsed the vague silhouettes of sailing vessels along the horizon, just where the sea and sky blend together?

Or is it two and a half centuries too late?

Time was when sailing vessels were commonplace along the Grand Strand. They could be seen lying low in the distance, or sailing into Little River and Murrells Inlet with the incoming tide.

Some of them flew the black flag brandishing the dreaded skull and crossbones.

By the early 1700s large fleets of ships, loaded with skins, furs, and rice, sailed regularly from Carolina ports like Charleston and Wilmington, bound for England. While these cargoes were not as rich as the gold and silver treasures of Central and South America, they were not ignored. Records show that the coves and inlets of the Grand Strand, from Southport and Calabash to Murrells Inlet and Georgetown, often harbored ships and men engaged in "larceny at sea," as the British termed it. The pirates carried on a brisk sale of black-market goods with some Coastal towns.

Along the North Carolina coast and in Charleston, as well, pirates often had the upper hand. Their ships were swift and well-armed. They threatened officials and made deals for shore privileges. Colonists welcomed the opportunity to buy needed goods without paying the king's taxes.

Piracy was considered a patriotic service to England, as long as the privateers and buccaneers attacked the ships of Spain and other countries. If an English ship was attacked, everything changed—it became the twin crimes of piracy and treason, both punishable by hanging.

Once such attacks had been made, there was no turning back for the pirates. They were wanted men, with a hefty price on their heads.

The coastline of the Carolina colonies proved to be a convenient refuge. Even the most wicked and bloodthirsty of men needed fresh water and supplies, and a place to rest and repair their boats. They brought their ships into the narrow, shallow swashes of the Grand Strand. Careening, or leaning the wooden ship against a sandy bank, made it easy to scrape, repair, or caulk the hull. When ready to sail again, the ship could be floated out on the high tide.

How could the people of the small weak settlements fight the pirates, or keep them out? Even the port cities of Wilmington and Charleston were attacked and terrorized when they tried to resist.

The British navy patrolled the North American coast out beyond the continental shelf, with some success, but the pirates knew all the little swashes and inlets, the deep channels, and the tiny little ports where they could lie low and rest.

It is estimated that about two thousand pirates thrived on the rich trade of the American Colonies in the early 1700s. Of these, only a few names are remembered. Possibly, the exploits of many were considered the acts of the best-known pirates.

When the British navy stepped up their activity, they captured hundreds who sailed under the "jolly roger" flag. Shute's Folly, located in Charleston harbor and now known as Castle Pinckney, was the place many captured pirates faced their execution. Records from one month in 1718 show that forty-nine cutthroats were hanged on Shute's Folly. Their crimes included blackmailing authorities, kidnapping citizens, capturing fleets of merchant ships, and robbing and murdering their victims.

Stede Bonnet, the "gentleman pirate," was captured in the mouth of a creek flowing into the Cape Fear River, in the port of Wilmington. The creek is still known as Bonnet's Creek. He surrendered after a nine-hour battle with Colonel William Rhett of Charleston. Bonnet and his men were hanged in December, 1718. Although he had cruelly forced his victims to walk the plank, Bonnet went to his own death trembling and whimpering.

Pirates lived violently and died violently. Captain William Lewis, after terrorizing the Carolina coast for ten years, was murdered in his sleep by his own men. His sadistic, ruthless acts had included members of his crew.

Captain George Lowther and his crew attacked shipping up and down the coast for many years. He was finally defeated in a battle with the British navy. Abandoning his ship and crew, he swam ashore and disappeared into the thick, jungle-like swamps near the Carolina coast. He died in the swamps, by his own hand.

One of the youngest pirates, Christopher Moody, lay in wait for ships off the Grand Strand. He later preyed upon the ships of Spain and Portugal along the shores of West Africa. He was captured in 1722 and hanged.

Anne Bonney, the daughter of a Carolina planter from Ireland, grew up in Charleston and Goose Creek. At sixteen she ran away with a sailor. The two of them joined pirates in the Caribbean. Anne became as wild and ruthless as any cutthroat. She encouraged fellow pirates to raid the Carolina coast, and killed her opponents in battle with a dagger. Captured and tried in Jamaica, she was found guilty

Anne Bonney
Courtesy of the North Carolina Division of Archives and History

of piracy, but was never hanged. She disappeared, though one story says she lived the rest of her life in Charleston as the mistress of a wealthy estate.

Richard Worley was considered one of the most bloodthirsty of all the pirates. He was also the most ambitious, capturing larger and larger ships, while abandoning smaller ships that were damaged in battle or not needed. He and his crew were captured by a fleet commanded by South Carolina Governor Robert Johnston. Worley went to the gallows in Charleston.

Edward Teach, better known as Blackbeard, ranks as one of the most infamous pirates of all time. He was a massive man with a bushy black beard, and his appearance struck terror in the hearts of his victims. With his large fleet of ships, he preyed on the rich South Carolina trade. He would then retreat to bays and inlets or island hideaways, where he could not be found. Once he captured nine ships in Charleston harbor, demanding a chest of medicine as a ransom.

After this event, Blackbeard received a pardon from North Carolina Governor Charles Eden. He even married a young girl and lived in a house in Bath, North Carolina for a while. But he couldn't resist the lure of piracy. Finally the governor of Virginia ordered warships to attack his headquarters on Ocracoke Island. In November, 1718, Blackbeard died in a battle with Lieutenant Maynard. His reign of terror along the Carolina coast finally ended.

Numerous pirates attacked ships off the Grand Strand. Since they often came ashore for rest and repairs, sometimes they buried treasure in remote or deserted areas, or on nearby islands. The treasure may still be there. As often as not, the pirates were never able to return.

A tale of Murrells Inlet involves a pirate named "Drunken Jack."

He sailed with Blackbeard. On one successful voyage their ship grew overloaded with one of the most prized trophies of the Caribbean, casks of prime rum. Blackbeard steered into Murrells Inlet, one of his favorite hideouts, to temporarily stash the booty. The pirates worked hard to bury most of the casks on an island, then celebrated with a feast of oysters and shrimp, along with all the rum they could drink. It turned into a wild night.

The next day the pirates awoke, groaning and retching. They staggered to their ship and sailed away. No one noticed Jack wasn't with them. He had fallen asleep the night before under some myrtle bushes and dry scrub palmetto, and didn't wake up with the others. Blackbeard and the crew missed Jack when their heads cleared a little, but by then they were too far out at sea to go back for him. They headed south for the Caribbean.

Two years later Blackbeard brought the ship back into Murrells Inlet to retrieve the rum. Instead they found on the island empty casks, thirty-two of them, scattered over the beach. Nearby, under the myrtle bushes, lay the bleached bones of a man. They assumed it was Jack, that he had lived and died in a drunken stupor. Drunken Jack's Island lies opposite the present Murrells Inlet sign, south of the village. A popular restaurant across the cove on the mainland keeps his name alive.

Other stories and rumors support the opinion that buried riches exist and might still be found. One farmer near the coast began to buy more land at a time when few people had any money to spend. His neighbors said one of his sons had discovered a pirate chest of coins under a river bluff. The rumor was never disproved.

Little River and Murrells Inlet were favorite hideouts for pirates. Is there treasure there?

To give credence to the legends, pirate maps appear from time to time. The maps mark places along the coast where pirates landed, visited, or buried valuables.

It might be fun to look for treasure during a Grand Strand vacation.

4

Murrells Inlet

Giant, moss-draped oak trees spread their branches over houses and yards. Tall old homes line the creek. Fishing boats put out to sea as they have for centuries. Old stories are told again and again, delighting each generation.

This is Murrells Inlet.

Here, ghosts of the past are friendly neighbors. Alice of the Hermitage still searches for her lost ring, while Theodosia of Brookgreen walks the garden trails near her plantation home. Drunken Jack still looks for his ship to return for him. Don't forget Blackbeard and the other pirates. Buried treasure may yet be found.

Claude Henry Neuffer, in his book *Names in South Carolina,* says there are continuing disputes over the naming of Murrells Inlet.

As early as 1715, there were people living in coastal inlets, bays, and swashes. These were fishermen, pirates, adventurers, or escaped criminals. A few people settled down to farm the rich soil and enjoy the mild climate. Many fishermen became part-time farmers, and claimed land. The inlet was known as Heston Bay.

One legend says a pirate named Captain John Murrell used the inlet as his headquarters, as pirates often did, while he preyed on ships at sea. To survive, local settlers had to trade with the pirates and help them obtain food and fresh water. When one of the ships Captain Murrell attacked had people from the inlet on board, he rescued them and carried them safely home. Thankful for having their lives spared, the victims rewarded the pirate with gifts of rice and named their settlement for him.

Another version of the story claims Captain Murrell was a fisherman and a trader, not a pirate, and that he rescued the inlet people from a sinking ship. In 1730, a Captain John Murrell bought a tract of land stretching from the Waccamaw River to the ocean, in the Richmond Hill area of Wachesaw. It is currently being excavated by archaeology students from Coastal Carolina University. In 1770 the land was divided among the captain's three children, and sold fifty years later to Dr. John McGill. Members of the Murrell family still live in Horry and Georgetown Counties.

Cherry Grove Inlet was also called Murrells Inlet. Both inlets may have been named for the Morrall family, who received extensive land grants near the coast in the 1700s. A John Morrall lived in Waccamaw Neck by 1750, and his son or grandson lived in Murrells Inlet in the early 1800s. Early plats of their land called it Morralls Inlet.

The inlet later became part of Laurel Hill Plantation, which was purchased with three other plantations to become Brookgreen Gardens in the 1930s.

Robert Mills added to the name confusion in 1825 when his *Atlas of South Carolina* was published. He called the area Murray's Inlet, which had no connection to a known family.

Edward B. Latimer, attorney for the Wildlife Resources Department of South Carolina, says the name of the community and post office should be Morrall's Inlet. He received the name from the U.S. Board of Geographic Names. Be that as it may, the post office and the village still use Murrells Inlet.

Many small islands in the inlet have interesting names: Goat

Island, Drunken Jack's Island, and Weston Mud Flats. Creek names include Conch, Clam, Shark Bend, Parsonage, Corner, Whale, and Woodland.

Perhaps descendants of the Murrell family prefer to think of their ancestor as a fisherman, trader, and landowner. Or maybe they prefer the story of the swashbuckling pirate with the kind heart, roaming the high seas, sailing in to the quiet cove for a time of rest from his adventures.

5

The Rice Culture

The slap of salty waves against the ship alerted Captain John Thurber to the rising of the tide. It was early morning, and his eyes roved over the lush green islands that appeared to enclose a large harbor. He planned to enter the harbor with the high tide, and hopefully find help.

Captain Thurber knew that Englishmen had settled along the coast and called their colony "Carolina," in honor of King Charles II. But was this the place? Or would he sail into a pirate lair, or something worse?

The sturdy vessel, carrying a cargo of long-grain rice from Madagascar to England, had been blown off course. The captain realized he needed repairs and supplies. About mid-morning his ship entered the harbor with the flag of England flying high, and dropped anchor some distance from shore. Then the captain and the crew waited to see what type of reception they would get.

A small boat left the shore and rowed toward the ship. It pulled alongside, and some men came on board. A man named Henry Woodward welcomed Thurber and his crew to the settlement of Charles Town. The ship had found friends.

Woodward had been a leader of the new colony since its establishment in 1670. During the days that followed, John Thurber and his crew were impressed with the kindness and hospitality of Woodward and others in the little village. When his ship had been repaired and provisioned, the captain gave a gift from his ship's cargo to his new friend, Henry Woodward: a bag of gold-seed rice.

Woodward shared the seed with the other planters and they began to experiment with the growing of rice. They found that the crop flourished in the Low Country tidewater region, where the ebb and flow of the tides affected the rivers for thirty miles inland. The fresh water could be used to flood the rice fields, an important part of cultivation.

With its countless creeks and wide rivers, the coastal plain was ideal for this method of farming. The planting of rice spread throughout the fertile area, and north to Georgetown and Waccamaw Neck. In a short time much of the wealth of the planters and of the colony was based on the rice culture.

Producing the rice crop carried with it a heavy work load. First, thousands of acres of swamps had to be drained and cleared of trees and stumps; the sheer magnitude of this job, performed by the slaves, compares with the building of the Egyptian pyramids. Then the slaves were trained to take care of the fragile, grass-like plants. Seedlings, transplanted from rich seedbeds of liquid mud, were planted in the fields by the men and women who waded through the mire. The ground around the small plants was kept soft by raking, or "hoeing with the toes." Often weeds grew faster than the rice plants, and had to be systematically pulled out.

Ocean tides pushed the fresh water of streams into shallow ditches, supplying the fields as the plants grew. "Watergates" across the ditches had to be monitored and closed to keep out salt water. Slave boys were often given this job. Perched precariously on top of the gate, the small boy would taste a handful of water from time to time. When he detected a brackish or salty taste, he would close the gate.

Another method of testing was to dip a piece of lye soap in the water. As long as it lathered, the water was fresh; soap would not lather in salt water. The little boys who monitored the gates lived in fear of "cooties" (cooters) or snakes nipping their toes, so they could be trusted to stay awake.

In the beautiful manor houses on the great plantations, an elaborate lifestyle developed, based on the rice crop's value as an export. South from Charleston to Beaufort, and north to Georgetown and Waccamaw Neck, plantation life rivaled that of the great estates of English nobility. The palatial homes were built with special attention to fine details. Ornate furnishings first came from overseas, but craftsmen in the colonies began to design and make similar products.

Large groups of slaves worked as field hands under overseers, but the house servants and a select group of slaves learned other skills. Each plantation was almost self-sufficient, with its own carpenters, blacksmiths, bricklayers, weavers, seamstresses, and silversmiths. Some plantations had their own silver design for flatware and serving pieces, named for the plantation.

In the kitchens, separated from the main house, black iron ladles and other tools were used for stirring and dipping food from the pots. The special rice spoon was used to serve mounded portions of the delicious hot rice, which had quickly become a favorite dish. The large silver serving spoon, called "the hospitality spoon," is still a gracious serving piece, especially in the South.

Gone from the South Carolina coastal area are the wide green rice fields, stretching into the distance like emerald lakes. No more do small boys monitor the watergates for the tidal influx of the killing salt water, or yank up their feet and peer into the murky water for cooters and snakes. No one hears a whisper of song from weary slaves, "hoeing with their toes," as they work in the rice fields under the watchful eye of the overseer.

Rice is no longer a crop in South Carolina.

Here and there a beautiful manor house still stands proudly on a rise above rich lawns and gardens, facing the river. Others are ghost houses, burned or neglected skeletons of buildings, abandoned and almost forgotten. A guide on a riverboat might recall the name of a plantation, or point out a narrow ditch from an old rice field. These are remnants of the unique way of life that developed in the Colonial South.

6

Goss's Inlet

The name of the big swash was Gause's Inlet, but soft slow accents slurred the pronunciation. Today there are sixty Gause families listed in Horry County, and the name is often pronounced "Goss." The inlet has been called White Point Creek and Swash since 1928.

The swash, lying along the south boundary of Windy Hill Beach, has a narrow coastal inlet, but it widens as it flows inland. East of Highway 17, the swash is the natural habitat of countless kinds of birds, fish, shell fish, and marsh grasses. West of the road, the tidal flow has been blocked to allow fresh water lakes for scenic value in the configuration of shops, restaurants, walkways, and streets along the waterway.

Although the swash has been protected east of the highway, the bacteriological count is high. Fishing is only allowed in the mouth of the inlet. Run-off water from storm drainage and land development causes contamination, but White Point waters compare favorably with other coastal swashes.

The name "Gause's Inlet" goes back to the 1730s. William Gause of Edgecomb County in eastern North Carolina had received a royal land grant of 250 acres between the Waccamaw River and the coast. Gause probably thought he was leaving his scant acreage in North Carolina for a rich lowland estate. He might have envisioned becoming a wealthy planter. He was doomed to disappointment.

Bringing his large family and all his possessions, Gause came to the Grand Strand in 1737 to claim his land. To his dismay, he found low, marshy land, "unfit for man or beast." His grant included the large inlet and swash, the drainage land marked with creeks, rills, oyster and clam beds, and thick marsh grasses. He noted an abundance of fish and game and the soft mild climate.

Gause's main concern was being able to feed his family. They all worked together to clear a few acres for food crops: corn, peas, beans, and potatoes for the family, and hay for the animals. Then Gause and his sons built a large dwelling on the highest point of his acreage. He decided to open a Public House (an inn) for travelers on the King's Highway.

At that time the highway was little more than an old Indian path in some places, but it was the only road between Wilmington and Georgetown, both important river towns on the coast. Gause's Inn and Tavern was a welcome stop for the occasional travelers.

When President George Washington planned his historic Southern Tour in 1791, he asked about accommodations along the sparsely traveled coast. His plans included stops in Wilmington, Georgetown, and Charleston, so the most direct route followed the King's Highway. Washington's secretary, Major Jackson, had traveled the coastal road before the American Revolution, and he remembered staying at Gause's Inn. As it turned out, the president stayed with a Mr. Vareen near Windy Hill. The group left early the next morning so they could cross Gause's Inlet and Singleton's Swash at low tide. The president noted in his journal that he had thought to stay at a tavern, probably William Gause's Public House.

Methodist Bishop Francis Asbury, in Volume II of his carefully-kept journal, told of visits and overnight stays with William Gause in 1796, 1799, 1801, and 1802. Asbury spoke of "his dear friend

William Gause, Senior," or "father William Gause," or the "patriarch of the place," all indicating that Gause lived to an old age. On Asbury's last visit, dated January 6, 1802, he found the old man had died.

Gause's original land grant has changed hands several times.

In 1965 entertainer Arthur Smith and his associates leased the property where Gause's Inn once stood and built a restaurant on the same hill. At that time it wasn't unusual to catch sight of alligators in the creek and razorback hogs roaming the thick woods nearby. Today White Point Restaurant occupies the site of the first inn, continuing the tradition of serving travelers which was begun by William Gause over two and a half centuries ago. Barefoot Traders, Inc. has grown rapidly into a complex of shops, restaurants, and theaters, one of the Grand Strand's major tourist attractions.

One wonders what William Gause would think of his "worthless land grant" today.

Look quickly as you drive past White Point Swash and Inlet, east of the King's Highway. It is still a living, teeming swash, beautiful to see, with grasses and reeds, herons and cranes and wild birds of all kinds, feeding on the pickings of the marsh. The area is a Mecca for bird watchers, in spite of nearby development that almost surrounds the inlet. Hopefully, it will continue to be a natural habitat.

The living, teeming White Point Swash

7

Grand Strand Names

Ever wondered about the strange names you see on signs and maps of the Grand Strand? Here are the stories behind a few of those names.

Lockwood's Folly Inlet and River lies about fifteen miles above the state line, east of Shallotte, North Carolina. It has kept its unusual name for over three hundred years, although it was named for a settler who dared not stay long. Following a failed settlement attempt along the Cape Fear River in 1663, Captain Lockwood, an adventurous Barbadian, brought a shipload of settlers in the 1670s. Lockwood entered the smaller river inlet farther south by mistake, his first "folly." He then lodged and wrecked his ship in the narrow river. He had to abandon it, along with the supplies, leaving the colonists with no safe haven. Lockwood demanded help from the native Indians; he mistreated them and caused them to attack. The settlers had to flee on foot. Lockwood antagonized his own group with his errors, violent temper, and poor judgment. He established no colony, and history branded him a "man of folly." The name stuck. A community, housing development, golf course, and the river and inlet continue to bear Lockwood's name.

Just north of the state line, the little fishing village of Calabash has become nationally famous for its seafood restaurants. In fact, the term "Calabash-style seafood" is used widely to describe a special method of food preparation. Fresh seafood (the day's catch, if possible) is lightly breaded and quickly deep-fried for a culinary treat. In 1940 people began "goin' to Calabash" to eat oysters roasted on an outside fire. The restaurant business soon followed.

President George Washington passed through in 1791 on the King's Highway. When his entourage stopped, he tied his horse to a young tree. A local legend says this is the reason a huge oak tree near the traffic light still tilts westward.

The little coastal river is shaped like a crooked-neck gourd, which the Indians called a *calabash*. Jimmy Durante once ate choice seafood at the Original Calabash Restaurant. Following that visit, he began to close his television show with his famous phrase, "Good night, Mrs. Calabash, wherever you are!" No one knows for sure what he meant, but it gave the village a lot of free publicity.

Waties Island was named for William Waties, an Indian trader in the early 1700s. Across Hog Inlet lies Cherry Grove Point, named for the groves of wild cherry trees found there.

The wide, hard, sandy strand of Ocean Drive encouraged people to drive or even race their cars close to the ocean. The obvious danger in parking on the beach lay in misjudging the rising tide and getting stuck in the soft sand. More than one car has had to spend the night there.

Crescent Beach describes the gradual curve of the beautiful strand. Atlantic Beach honors the name of the ocean and remained a separate town when other beaches joined to form North Myrtle Beach.

According to tradition, President George Washington named Windy Hill while spending the night there with Jeremiah Vareen. He commented, "My! What a windy hill!"

Myrtle Beach, first called "New Town," was named for the native wax myrtle bushes growing close to the sand dunes. From Singleton Swash to Withers Swash, the unbroken strand was characterized by President Washington in his journal as "Long Beach of the Ocean."

South of Hurl Rocks, a section of coastline is identified as Yaupon Beach on some old maps. It was named for the thick growth of native yaupon bushes and trees, with their bright red winter berries. Indians used the poisonous berries in coming-of-age ceremonies for their young men to prove their manhood. They were given gourds full of bitter tea made from the crushed berries. It was a test of their courage and stamina to drink the tea and retain it as long as possible before retching and vomiting. Young braves often died proving their manhood.

Huntington Beach and State Park was first called Magnolia Beach, but changed to its present name for the benefactors of Brookgreen Gardens.

Some names have changed several times. Surfside Beach was a part of Roaches' plantation, and first known as Roaches Beach. Next it was called the Old Ark, for an old house that withstood numerous storms. When the Holiday family purchased the area, they named it Floral Beach for Mrs. Holiday of Galivants Ferry, South Carolina. Finally in the 1950s, the name Surfside Beach was decided upon.

Debidue comes from the French surname *Debourdieu.* Another story says that shipwrecked people reached the shore and gave thanks to the mercy of God, "*De bon Dieu.*"

Above: Withers Lake; Below: The high sand hill overlooking the lake
where Francis Withers built his doomed plantation house in the 1700s

8

Withers Swash

Withers Swash lies along Third Avenue South, entering the ocean on a stretch known as Spivey Beach. The swash flows beside the Swamp Fox Roller Coaster and back of Quincy's Steak House into a large lake, bounded by Fifth Avenue South and Charlotte Road. There the swash narrows to a stream and follows Third Avenue to cross Highway 501, parallel Canal Street, and curve beside Tenth Avenue North toward Highway 17. As a bush and trash-filled ditch, it drains a large part of central Myrtle Beach.

Before 1970 the swash was a clean, beautiful tidal creek and lake. Children waded and learned to swim in the clear salty water, chasing the birds that pecked for food in the luxuriant marsh grasses. The lake and swash teemed with fish, shrimp, and crabs.

Today Withers Swash lies contaminated and trash-laden, its waters dark and murky. It has the poorest water quality of any marsh along the Grand Strand. Its fragile ecology has been destroyed.

In the 1700s Withers Swash was part of a 66,000-acre land grant to Robert Francis Withers, who owned several plantations near Georgetown. He built a large plantation house for his family on "a bold bluff overlooking the swash." That bluff, somewhat weathered and worn down, may be viewed from a parking lot just north of Fifth Avenue South. The house faced the beautiful lake. Fields south and west of the house were planted in indigo before the Revolution.

Francis Withers and other members of his family are buried in Withers Cemetery, located on First Avenue and Collins Street.

The Withers house died a violent death. In 1822 a powerful hurricane came ashore after three days of heavy rains, and the storm surge coincided with the high tide. The water rushed in as far as the Withers' house, thought to be safe on its hill. Eighteen people had taken refuge inside. A sudden surge of water lifted the house off its foundation and floated it into the swash and out to sea. The windows shone brightly with the light of candles and lamps, making it look like a ship sailing away. The house finally broke up and everyone inside lost their lives. A legend says that on wild, stormy nights, the lighted house can sometimes be seen floating down the swash and out to sea.

The Withers family abandoned their land holdings, which were later sold to Joshua John Ward. The large acreage had included most of what is now Myrtle Beach. With the house gone, the fields grew up in pine and scrub oak trees.

However, the Withers name was not forgotten. It is used for a street, a cemetery, and Withers Big Swamp, as well as the swash. On April 30, 1888 the first area post office, located near the swash, opened with the name Withers, South Carolina. With the building of the railroad, Myrtle Beach Post Office opened May 21, 1901, and the Withers Post Office closed in September 1901.

There is reason to hope Withers Swash can be brought back to its former beauty and cleanliness. Myrtle Beach City Council has gone ahead with plans to rescue the swash from its present state. With the cooperation of residents, business, and government, the swash may once again run with clear water and teem with wildlife.

9

Little River

Indian tribes roaming the coastal plain called the stream *Mineola*, meaning "little river," and that became its name. The town of Little River was one of the earliest settlements along the coast, with a few farmers, fishermen, traders, and shipwreck survivors coming to stay in the early 1700s. They settled on a wide, salt tidal inlet, which narrows to a stream. The river became part of the Intracoastal Waterway when it opened for traffic in 1936. Still a small picturesque village, Little River takes pride in its historic past, even as it faces the extensive growth and development of today.

The first settlers gave shelter and aid to pirates, as many coastal settlements had to do. Names like Captain Kidd, Blackbeard, and Anne Bonney are part of the local lore. From time to time, maps appear that attempt to locate buried pirate treasure.

According to the highway marker south of Little River, Reverend George Whitefield, fiery "Oxford Methodist," visited the village in 1740. Reverend Whitefield saw the villagers celebrating New Year's Day with music, dancing, and spirits. He chastised them, and the partying stopped. The villagers listened to the reverend, some nodding, some hanging their heads. When Whitefield left, they continued their celebrating.

Settlers were slow in coming to Horry County; large land grants brought a few families. Names like Bellamee (Bellamy), Gause,

Allston, Varin (Vareen), Vaught, Lewis, and Bessent go back to the 1700s. In 1791 George Washington, on his tour of the South, ate his midday meal with a Revolutionary War veteran named James Cochran in Little River. Descendants of these families still live in Horry County.

The Robert Mills Atlas of Horry District, South Carolina, 1828, lists Little River and Conwayborough as the only two villages in the county. Both settlements offered few jobs to attract newcomers. Travel between the two was difficult because of marshy land and river swamps.

Until recently the gaunt burned structure of a fine old house, its massive end chimneys still pointing toward the sky, towered over the grassy slope near the harbor in Little River. It was the Randall-Vereen House, considered the oldest remaining house in Horry County until it burned. The house was one of three built by Captain Thomas Randall of New England, who came to Little River soon after The War of 1812. For a time, people called Little River "Yankee Town" because a few people from New England had come to live there.

Northern markets wanted the fine lumber and naval stores produced from the rich stands of native pine in Horry County. Little River became a prosperous port, with a large sawmill, warehouse, stores, churches, school, and a bank. The Civil War wiped out this progress. A large salt works produced the much needed commodity for the Confederate army, until Union soldiers burned the facility.

Seagoing steamers, loaded with cargo and passengers, made regular runs in the late 1800s between Wilmington, Little River, and Georgetown.

Little River also played host to pirates, smugglers, Civil War blockade-runners, and drug dealers in modern times. With road building in the 1920s and cars and trucks to carry people and products, sea traffic diminished.

Today, Little River is widely known for its deep-sea fishing tournaments, charter boats, and commercial fishing. Visitors come to watch the fleets of fishing and shrimping boats go out for the day's catch, to supply restaurants and fish markets.

The Blue Crab Festival in the spring expands the population overnight from four thousand to about fifty thousand. Taking place the weekend after Mother's Day, the festival features arts and crafts booths, stages with continuous entertainment, a petting zoo, clowns, puppets, strolling musicians, and other attractions. The food booths present some of the best cuisine the Grand Strand has to offer, including mountains of steaming blue crabs, king of the festival.

Little River continues to grow, yet massive oak trees still frame fine old homes, with traditional porches that invite visitors to come in and sit a while.

General Peter Horry

10

Horry County and the American Revolution

A scant forty years after the first settlers came to Horry (Kingston), rumblings of discontent and rebellion spread through the American Colonies. The royal government in Charleston had offered little help to the struggling settlers in Kingston-on-the-Waccamaw, and attitudes were mostly anti-British from the beginning.

But the nature of the conflict meant that any stranger would be viewed with suspicion. Only when he revealed sympathy for the American cause would he be accepted.

The Boundary House, built on the North Carolina-South Carolina line, was the home of Isaac Marion, Justice of the Peace and brother of Francis Marion. Twenty days after the Battle of Lexington and Concord in Massachusetts, in 1775, a courier arrived at the Boundary House with news of the fighting. In 1776 news of the Declaration of Independence came by post rider to the Boundary House. Messengers set out for Kingston and other settlements.

Young men rushed to join the Patriot fighters. American General Francis Nash, on a march from Wilmington to Charleston, camped for several weeks with 9,000 troops on Little River Neck.

The Marquis de Lafayette first landed in America near Georgetown. He was a wealthy French nobleman, heir to a prestigious title and extensive estates. He had studied at the Military Academy of

France at Versailles, and been commissioned a captain of cavalry at age seventeen. He loved the American determination for liberty, and admired George Washington, so he gathered a group of young Frenchman, all trained soldiers, and left France in March, 1777. The French king opposed their going to America, so they sailed secretly. The Baron de Kalb sailed with them.

Lafayette intended to land at Philadelphia, but the ship was blown off course and sailed into Winyah Bay. The group went ashore on North Island. They reached Major Benjamin Huger's summer home on June 14, 1777. Fortunately Huger supported the American rebels. Being a Frenchman and a traditional English enemy, Lafayette would have received harsh treatment from the Redcoats. Huger supplied the men with food and horses, and directed them north on the King's Highway.

The men commented on the beauty of the Grand Strand, although they watched vigilantly to avoid British patrols at sea. It took them weeks to cross the Grand Strand and travel through the swamps of North Carolina and Virginia, but they reached Philadelphia safely. Lafayette and Baron de Kalb, with their military experience, trained and led troops in the Continental army. Lafayette became almost a son to General Washington.

At Bear Bluff on the Waccamaw River, two small detachments of Patriots from Kingston and Little River caught a group of Tories between them. The men on the opposing sides came from neighboring farms, and carried whatever guns they had at home. The Tories, seeing themselves outnumbered and trapped, threw their guns into the river and ran. Some dove into the water to escape.

Another fight between a handful of Tories and Patriots took place at Black Creek, along the Pee Dee River. The skirmish produced no significant results.

General Francis Marion, the Swamp Fox, led daring raids against the British, then disappeared into the river marshes. His soldiers used bird or animal calls to signal to each other. Marion's main camp was on Snow Island, in the Pee Dee River. Men from the Kingston District fought with him, as well as with other partisan groups, and the American armies under George Washington and Nathaniel Greene.

Many Tories, despised and misused by the British regular army leaders, later joined the American forces.

In nearby Georgetown, British soldiers desecrated Prince George Winyah Church, stabling their horses in the classic old building.

The end of the Revolution in 1781 brought a new state government, with John Rutledge as governor. In 1785 Kingston became a separate district or county, instead of part of Georgetown District. It was called Kingston County, and the little Kingston settlement became the county seat and courthouse town.

In 1801 the county name was changed to honor General Peter Horry of Georgetown. Horry, aide to Francis Marion, fought in a skirmish at Waccamaw Neck, near Pawley's Island. When a British patrol attacked an American patrol, Horry and the rest of his men rushed into the battle, forcing the British to withdraw.

Peter Horry stood well over six feet tall and weighed about three hundred pounds. The owner of several plantations, he gave his time, money, and considerable strength to the struggle for independence. He suffered from a lifelong speech impediment. *Anecdotes of the Revolutionary War* by Major Alexander Garden, published in 1822, tells of Peter Horry in the Battle of Quinby. Horry set his detachment for an ambush of the British. He waited until the Redcoats were almost upon them before giving the order to fire. Except he couldn't get the order out. He tried five times, until red with frustration, he yelled, "Shoot, damn you, shoot! You know very well what I would say! Shoot! Shoot! And be dam'd to you!"

Horry later served as militia commander and in the South Carolina General Assembly. His diary provided valuable insight into the Southern theater of the Revolutionary War, and an interesting commentary on Carolina society during those years.

After the Revolution, Horry County expected and received as little help from the new government as they had from the British. Cut off from the rest of the state by the Pee Dee, Lumber, and Waccamaw rivers, with no bridges, residents took care of themselves. They farmed, carried on business, settled disputes and punished crimes, all with no outside help. They later even referred to their county as the Independent Republic of Horry. The Horry County Historical Society publication, *The Independent Republic Quarterly*, continues to use the name.

Kingston's name was changed to Conwayborough, honoring General Robert Conway, who also fought in the Revolution and owned land in the Waccamaw River settlement. (In 1883 the South Carolina General Assembly shortened the town's name to Conway.)

The new names, Horry and Conwayborough, cut all eighteenth-century ties with the king of England. A new nation had taken root.

11

Hurl Rocks

An unusual formation of rocks lies along the shore near 20th Avenue South, about two miles below the pavilion and amusement park in Myrtle Beach. Hurl Rocks was familiar to fishermen and picnickers from the early days of settlement along the Grand Strand.

Several years before the American Revolution, an Englishman named Hearl landed in Georgetown and made his way up the Waccamaw River to the tiny settlement of Kingston. Mr. Hearl reached Kingston on Friday. He went across the river toward the beach with some new-found friends on Saturday. Never one to let grass grow under his feet, he met a woman and married her on Sunday. The marriage may have been performed by a circuit-riding preacher who would not be making his rounds for another three months.

Hearl claimed a homestead in Socastee, a farming community located east of the Waccamaw River, about halfway between Kingston and the beach. He and his wife had several daughters and one son; some of their descendants still live in Horry County. It was customary in the eighteenth century to name a landmark for the family living closest to it. Since the Englishman's homestead was nearest the rocks, they received his name.

Colonial botanist John Bartram, in his journal dated July 19, 1765, described the rocks as "a solid sheet of concreet—so soft as with a sharp knife to cut a little hole in it." He mentioned a deep red-orange color tingeing the rocks and cockle and clam shells. In Robert Mills' *Atlas of the Horry District in South Carolina*, 1838, the beds of rocks are identified as "fossiliferous rocks," commonly known as coquina, a soft limestone of broken shells and coral.

Hurl Rocks

A news item from the *Horry Herald* dated August 9, 1900, reads: "There will be a picnic at the Hearle Rocks tomorrow. We regret very much to have to refuse an invitation to be present. The people of Socastee know how to make you feel good."

In the early 1900s, some of the rocks stood three to six feet tall, a high point on the flat, sandy strand. Children always enjoyed climbing on the rocks and looking for the treasures brought in by the tides: colorful bits of shell and seaweed, a starfish or tiny seahorse, a sand dollar, or even debris from a shipwreck. With a little imagination, the top of the rocks might be the deck of a pirate ship, or the tower of a moated castle.

According to the late Florence Epps, founding editor of *The Independent Republic Quarterly,* property including the rocks was purchased in 1913 by her aunt, Margaret Ann Klein of New York City. The beach and the rocks were used by anyone who came by. Miss Klein liked to watch the tide come in. She noticed that the mass of the rock formation caused the water to divide and splash against the rocks more forcefully, with a colorful surging and cresting of the waves. Or, the water "hurled" itself against the rocks. She decided Hurl Rocks was a more descriptive name, and since she owned the property, she changed it.

In Myrtle Beach today, a parking area and a small city park mark the location known as Hurl Rocks. The Beach Renourishment Program has covered parts of the formation with heavy mounds of sand, but high tides and storms continually wash the sand away, revealing the timeless rocks to new groups of visitors.

12

The King's Highway

It was called "The King's Highway" from early Colonial times. Beginning in the 1600s, the king's couriers used the road in carrying directives to royal governments in coastal settlements. Post riders traveled periodically from Boston, Massachusetts to Charleston, stopping dozens of times along the way to drop off messages or pick up new ones. By the mid-1700s, the road had extended to the new settlement at Savannah, Georgia, just across the river. The road remained a tenuous overland link for news, mail, and travel.

It had its beginnings as a narrow Indian path, running close to the beach through pine thickets, native yaupon, myrtle, and bay trees. For countless centuries different Indian tribes used the trail in their seasonal migrations. Long before Spanish explorers or English settlers came, the trail skirted deep swashes and bays, except where deeper tidal inlets forced travelers farther inland.

Today U. S. Highway 17 is often referred to as the Ocean Highway. In many areas, among them the Grand Strand, it is also called the King's Highway. The road still runs parallel to the coast for its entire length, from New England to Florida. It is probably the most level highway in the East, varying from nine to fifteen feet above sea level. In South Carolina, the road stretches 234.6 miles from the North Carolina line to the Savannah River, the boundary with Georgia.

Just south of the North Carolina line, a highway marker points to the site of the Boundary House, built in 1754. The home of Isaac Marion stood near the tenth hole on the Marsh Harbor Golf Course, with the state line running directly through it.

Travelers in the 1700s called the King's Highway the "Georgetown Road" or the "Wilmington Road," depending on their destination. President George Washington followed the road on his Southern Tour in 1791, as he journeyed from Wilmington to Georgetown, and on to Charleston. In his journal he described the Grand Strand as "...sand and pine barrens, with very few inhabitants." It was a desolate route to travel, with few inns or houses to offer food or lodging.

One spot that even got listed on the map was a "refreshment Oak." A certain hollow oak tree near the King's Highway always had a jug of brandy in it. Weary travelers could stop and refresh themselves, with the understanding that they would replenish the jug on their return journey.

Swashes and inlets had to be forded with care at low tide. The sandy rutted King's Highway had no bridges, and the marshlands and tidal flows weren't suited to the use of flatboats or ferries. The first straightening and paving of the road began in 1927, with bridges built to cross the main inlets.

The Cooper River Bridge into Charleston opened in 1929. In 1935 Georgetown celebrated the opening of the Lafayette Bridge over the Waccamaw and Pee Dee rivers. Previous access to the historic port had been limited by the use of a ferry. The Lafayette Bridge forged the final link in the Ocean Highway for South Carolina.

News releases widely proclaimed the King's Highway to be the fastest and safest route for North-South travel. The increased flow of traffic played an important part in developing tourism in the Southeast. People just passing through noticed the beaches and climate.

The King's Highway today is a fine four-lane road from Wilmington to Jacksonboro, South Carolina, thirty miles south of Charleston. The highway passes through Myrtle Beach, but a bypass takes travelers around the main area. Just south of the city lies the most widely used state park in South Carolina. Across the highway is the former Myrtle Beach Air Force Base.

Passing Surfside Beach, Garden City, and the historic village of Murrells Inlet, the road leads to Huntington Beach State Park, across from Brookgreen Gardens, the world's largest statuary gardens.

Pawleys Island, a small island beach resort for plantation families in Colonial times, is still popular today. Side roads from the King's Highway lead to Waccamaw Neck plantations from the indigo and rice era, dating to the days before the Revolution. Country clubs, golf courses, and fine homes have been developed on many of the old plantations.

Farther south, the highway offers access to Georgetown, Charleston, Beaufort, Hilton Head, Port Royal, Parris Island, and newly developed resort areas. Crossing the Savannah River into Georgia, the highway runs down the coast into Florida, an alternate route for travelers who wish to leave Interstate 95.

Plan to take an unhurried journey along the King's Highway in South Carolina soon. It is one of the oldest roads in the United States in continuous use since Colonial Times. Stop to read the historical markers and explore the old towns and cities. Visit the shops and sample Low Country cooking while you listen to the tales of local residents. Take time to enjoy the serene beauty of South Carolina's regions, with its flowing rivers, giant moss-hung oaks, teeming marshlands, old abandoned rice fields, and memories of a bygone era.

13

Theodosia

In 1813 the poignant, bewildering question asked again and again was, "Where is Theodosia?"

Her young husband, the governor of South Carolina, waited on the docks at Georgetown, where she had boarded a small ship bound for New York. Often he stood gazing out across Winyah Bay, or talked to the men who worked on the docks. In Columbia he sat alone in his quarters, scarcely mindful of his duties.

In New York the dapper figure of an aging lawyer could be seen in the late afternoons making his way to the docks. Day after day for months, he stood, looking out to sea, awaiting the arrival of his beloved only daughter, Theodosia Burr Alston.

Nearly two hundred years later the question is still unanswered—what happened to Theodosia?

If Theodosia's troubled ghost walks the paths at Brookgreen Gardens, or sighs in the winds around the great oaks, how will she ever find the peace she deserved?

Born in 1783, Theodosia grew up in New York City. She was the only child of Aaron Burr and Theodosia Prevost Burr. Her mother died when she was only nine, and from that time her father considered her his hostess and housekeeper. She was his constant companion, and she idolized him.

Aaron Burr was a brilliant lawyer, a United States senator, and third vice-president, serving with President Thomas Jefferson after a highly contested election. Burr's many enemies called him "an infamous rascal." He entertained lavishly the scores of visitors who came to his New York home and to Richmond Hill, his estate near the city.

One of the visitors was a young attorney and rice planter from South Carolina, Joseph Alston. He had inherited his plantation, The Oaks, from his wealthy grandfather. Located between the Waccamaw River and the ocean, The Oaks was one of four plantations that today make up Brookgreen Gardens.

Theodosia at eighteen was considered one of the most beautiful and accomplished young women in the country. Her poise and intelligence dazzled everyone she met. Her father had carefully planned her education and helped her develop social graces and proficiency in music, French, Latin, and Greek. She and Joseph were attracted to each other at first sight. Her friends wondered what she saw in a young man from the wilds of Coastal Carolina, far from the social life of New York and the new capital city, Washington, D. C.

After a whirlwind courtship, Theodosia and Joseph were married in 1801, and came to the plantation in South Carolina. This move introduced the lovely, cultured New York girl to a way of life so different that she must have felt she was in another country. As the new mistress of the great one thousand-acre plantation, she assumed a variety of duties. She found herself responsible for the health and well-being of over two hundred slaves and their families, for her newly built home, and elaborate entertaining. The social life of the Waccamaw Neck rice planters and Georgetown required even more work than had her father's entertaining in New York. When the young couple visited their town house in Charleston, there were still more obligations to fulfill.

The idea of slavery greatly disturbed Theodosia. She understood the necessity of workers on a plantation, but she never accepted the right to own other human beings. No doubt she and Joseph frequently disagreed over the issue. To add to her troubles, the incredible heat and humidity of Low Country summers and bouts of fever left her frail and sickly, scarcely able to cope with her responsibilities.

Letters from her father offered advice and cheered her immensely, especially when Joseph spent time in Charleston looking after his affairs there. Burr advised his daughter to stay at Magnolia Beach (now Huntington State Park) which was part of their property. He suggested going to the mountains to escape the heat, and she did.

The only child of Theodosia and Joseph was born in 1802. They named their son Aaron Burr Alston, for his grandfather. He was a joy to everyone, including his grandfather who adored him.

In 1804 serious trouble struck Theodosia's beloved father. Aaron Burr shot and killed Alexander Hamilton in a duel. Public opinion immediately turned against him. Although dueling was legal, Burr faced the threat of a murder indictment, a shameful situation for the vice-president of the United States. Theodosia grieved for her father, and also for Hamilton's wife and children, whom she had known.

Burr survived that scandal, but then became involved in 1806 in a land scheme along the Mississippi River. He and Harman Blennerhasset were later accused of treason for a plot to take over land west of the river and set up another nation in American territory. They were tried in federal court in Richmond and acquitted. Theodosia, convinced her father could do no wrong, went to Richmond to support him. After the trial Burr sailed for France, where he spent four years in self-imposed exile. He had lost his property, his fortune, and nearly all of his friends.

Returning to New York in 1812, Burr learned horrible news: his ten year old grandson had died of fever. Theodosia and Joseph had buried their son in the family cemetery at The Oaks. They were stunned with grief.

Joseph, newly elected governor of South Carolina at age thirty-three, had duties that kept him in Columbia as another war with England erupted. He thought a visit to her father in New York might help Theodosia's grief and depression. Plans were made.

Late in December of 1812, Theodosia left Georgetown aboard *The Patriot* for the six-day voyage to New York. The small sailing vessel was never seen or heard from again.

Days and weeks passed with no word of *The Patriot.* Authorities searched the shipping lanes and ports from New York to the Bahamas, but found no evidence of the missing ship. Frantic letters were sent between Joseph and Burr. Theodosia had disappeared, never to return. The young governor never recovered from the loss of his wife and son, and died following a seizure in 1816. He was buried in the Alston family cemetery beside his son.

Numerous theories have surfaced about the fate of *The Patriot.* It may have sunk in a winter storm off Cape Hatteras, the "Graveyard of Ships." It may have been attacked by pirates, and the passengers forced to walk the plank. Or maybe it was lured onto the rocks and shoals of the Outer Banks of North Carolina by "Bankers," cutthroats who lived by salvaging the cargo of wrecked ships. In nearly two centuries no theory has been proven.

Some visitors to Brookgreen Gardens and the beach at Huntington State Park have said they felt the presence of Theodosia, searching for her husband and child. Perhaps she is trying to return from the ocean to her home at The Oaks.

Whether or not her ghost wanders, Theodosia's disappearance lives as a coastal mystery.

Entrance to the Alston family cemetery on The Oaks, where Theodosia's small son and heartbroken husband were buried

14

Along the Waccamaw River

"We crossed the Waggamau to Georgetown by descending the River three miles..." This entry in President George Washington's diary, dated April 30, 1791, tells of the journey of his entourage along the King's Highway through the Grand Strand area. A further note mentions that the river was at flood stage, a common April occurrence today.

The name given to the twisting river came from the tribe of Waccamaw Indians who lived along its banks. It is the most familiar and widely used Indian name in the region.

The gradual rise of the coastal plain extends inland up and down the eastern shore of the United States. In South Carolina the plain, called the Low Country, is flat and swampy. The land is subject to flooding, especially where forested areas have been cut and housing developments have wrested a location from the fragile environment. The plain is cut through by creeks, fast-flowing rivers, and arms of the sea called swashes. Ocean tides push the water up the rivers and creeks for thirty miles inland. This half-drowned area is known as the tidewater region of South Carolina.

The Waccamaw is a coastal river, rising in spring-fed Lake Waccamaw, located about thirty miles west of Wilmington, North Carolina. As the river winds south, it gathers strength from numerous small creeks and streams. Flowing through swamps, quicksand pits,

The Waccamaw River

freshwater lakes, and jungle-like growth, the river widens and deepens below Conway. The Intracoastal Waterway joins the wide Waccamaw near Bucksport. The combined river and waterway empty into Winyah Bay at Georgetown.

The term "over the river" had a real meaning to early settlers in Horry County. Travel was difficult. Private ferries began to operate on the Waccamaw in 1770, beginning with Wasso Ferry near Georgetown. Ferries were named for their location, or for the families operating them.

At first the ferries were shallow rafts, depending on long poles and muscle power. They were operated by family members, day or night, for a small fee. Bishop Francis Asbury was surprised to see women operating Hemingway Ferry at Savannah Bluff in 1801 and

1805, but it was common practice. Some of the ferries were later licensed by the state. Cable and pulley ferries replaced the pole-operated flats.

As the river flows south from Conway, it makes its way past Woodward's Landing, which was part of a large land grant to James Woodward in 1791. The Landing is near Toddville, a village built on the site of an old Indian town and burial ground.

Farther on, the remains of an old smokestack show the location of Upper Mill, the first of three lumber mills built after 1828 by Henry Buck of Bucksport, Maine. A beautiful old plantation house stands serenely on a bluff above the river, and still belongs to the Buck family.

Middle Mill, also known as Bucksville, was one of the largest lumber mills in the state in the 1800s. Pine and cypress from the Bucksville mill were shipped to New York for the building of the Brooklyn Bridge. Schooners from all over the world tied up at the extensive Bucksville docks. The proud sailing vessel *The Henrietta* was built at Bucksville in the 1870s. The ship, over two hundred feet long, had to be towed to Charleston for its rigging and sails. *The Henrietta* sailed the oceans of the world before sinking in a typhoon off the coast of Japan in 1894.

Road's End (Bucksport Plantation) and the riverfront docks were built by Jonathan Buck in 1838. The old house, now standing empty, has a nostalgic look reminiscent of New England, with its mossy gray shingles and Cape Cod style.

Bull Creek joins the Waccamaw and Pee Dee rivers about twelve miles south of Conway. The creek was used in years gone by for local trade and travel. The remnants of a little ghost town, Port Harrelson, can be seen on Bull Creek at Cowford Lake. The Charles Dusenbury house is the only home left from a thriving village that once had two churches and a school.

During the American Revolution, General Francis Marion, the Swamp Fox, and his men camped on Bull Creek and collected supplies from the plantations. Men from the lower part of Horry County met at Cowford Lake in 1861 to organize a company for the Confederate Army.

From the earliest days of settlement in Horry County, the river served as the main link with Georgetown and the outside world. Travel, trade, and mail all depended on the Waccamaw. A lively trade built up in the 1800s, with lumber from the saw mills, naval stores (tar and pitch) from the pine trees, shingles from cypress trees, and farm products.

During the Civil War all trade was geared to helping the Confederate war effort. Flatboats and barges filled the river. Local people saw their first steamboat in 1862. The *Francis Marion* steamed up the river from Georgetown to Conway to recruit more soldiers.

Two Union gunboats moved up the Waccamaw in May, 1862 as far as Izard Middleton's Mill on Arcadia Plantation. Poorly armed Confederate guards under Captain John Tucker of Litchfield Plantation opened fire on the gunboats. Even though the Confederates only had the rifles, shotguns, and pistols they personally owned, they made enough noise to convince the gunboats to turn back.

River trade slowed during the Reconstruction Period. By the late 1800s the trade picked up, helping the slow economy. Steamboats replaced some of the flatboats and barges. Regular service for passengers made travel between Conway and Georgetown more comfortable. From 1910 to 1920, steamboats went back and forth between the two towns every day. The building of railroads, better roads and bridges, and the coming of automobiles caused steamboat travel and trade to gradually disappear in the 1930s.

Steamships like the *Commanche* carried passengers up and
down the Waccamaw River just after the turn of the century
Courtesy of the Horry County Museum

One of the buildings still located on the banks of the river in
Conway was constructed in 1880 to be used as a riverboat terminal.
Some people in Horry County remember the days of steamboat
travel along the Waccamaw. Today, pleasure boats and dedicated
fishermen fill the river, especially in summer.

A few, widely-spaced bridges span the Waccamaw River today:

Highway 9 near Longs and North Myrtle Beach
Highway 47 at Red Bluff
Highway 501 Business and 501 at Conway
Highway 17 at Winyah Bay, Georgetown

Otherwise, travelers who cross the Waccamaw must either paddle or swim, since the ferries no longer operate.

Many modern, plantation-type homes have been built in recent years along the river north and south of Conway, and in the Toddville-Bucksville area. Some fine old homes have been restored. River land has again come into its own, despite the constant threat of flooding.

Conway's Riverfest, celebrated in the spring, emphasizes the importance of the Waccamaw River to the town and to the region.

15

Alice

Ghost of the Hermitage

Will Alice ever find contentment, or will she wander through the Hermitage and Murrells Inlet forever?

The Hermitage was built in the 1840s by Dr. Allard Belin Flagg, owner of Wachesaw Plantation. The two-story white house, with its twelve-foot ceilings, polished pine floors, and wide front porch overlooking the creek was to be the home of Dr. Flagg's widowed mother and his young sister, Alice. The surrounding grounds consisted of moss-hung trees, wild roses, wisteria vines, and grassy areas, all beautiful in any season.

From Alice's upstairs room she could see tidal waters washing across oyster beds, reeds, and marshes, with the blue Atlantic Ocean in the distance. She often stared out the window, dreaming of a handsome young man who lived nearby. A young man who loved her. He was not a member of the rich plantation society to which the Flaggs belonged, so their affair remained a secret. Alice sometimes rode her horse on the beach to clandestinely meet her love.

Dr. Flagg learned of her affair and swept Alice off to boarding school in Charleston, putting an end to the secret meetings. In Charleston, Alice grew ill with fever and a broken heart. Dr. Flagg came to take her home to the Hermitage. When they reached Murrells Inlet, the sick, unhappy young woman was unconscious.

Alice's grave

While she was being undressed and put to bed, Alice's engagement ring was discovered, hanging from a chain around her neck. Dr. Flagg's love and concern for his beautiful young sister instantly turned to bitter rage. Snatching the ring from her neck, he stalked outside and threw it as far as he could into the dark waters of the salt marsh.

As sick as she was, Alice knew her precious ring was missing. She moaned and cried for it. Her condition worsened. The doctor sat by her bed, helpless to save her. She died, begging with her last breath for her ring.

Since then, people have glimpsed a mysterious "lady in white," a lovely young woman wearing a white gown. The apparition seems to be searching for something.

In the All Saints' Parish, Waccamaw Cemetery lies a simple, flat gravestone, inscribed with one name–Alice. Most people believe it is the burial place of Alice Flagg, the lady in white of the Hermitage. But hers is a restless spirit, still looking for her ring after all these years. The trench worn around the gravestone shows how many people come, year after year, to see her grave, retell her story, and reluctantly peer through the trees for a glimpse of her ghost.

Mr. and Mrs. Clarke A. Willcox, Sr. of Marion, South Carolina purchased the Hermitage and moved there in 1910 with son Clarke, Jr., and daughter Genevieve.

Clarke, Jr., "Mr. Clarke," as everyone in Murrells Inlet called him, inherited the house. He collected and retold the sightings of Alice Flagg. His aunt once spent a night in Alice's room. When she looked in the mirror, Alice's ghostly face stared back at her.

Other family members and friends claimed to have seen the ghost. Some saw her in the upstairs front bedroom, on the stairs, along the creek and marsh, and in the cemetery. Some accounts have her moving slowly through the azaleas and camellias, looking for her lover's grave.

Mr. Clarke and his wife, Miss Lillian, often received guests on their spacious porch, repeating these stories and countless others, and showing the house to visitors interested in their resident ghost. Mr. Clarke said he never saw Alice, but he always knew she was close by. He died in 1989 at the age of 93. He is remembered as the "Ghost Story Curator of the Hermitage," and for his many poems and writings, including the book, *Musings of a Hermit.*

The Willcox's four daughters decided to move the classic old home to another part of the original plantation and sell the valuable waterfront property. The Hermitage is listed in the *National Register of Historic Places.*

The old house, filled with memories, sits dreaming on its new site at the end of Chandler Drive in Murrells Inlet. It is now the property of Joe Chandler, Mr. Clarke's nephew. He and his wife are restoring the house for their retirement home. It will no longer be open to the public.

Perhaps Alice moved with the Hermitage. Or perhaps you'll meet her in Murrells Inlet on some dark, lonely night.

16

The Earthquake of 1886
"The Great Cool Spring Shake"

"I was awakened by a terrible noise. The house seemed to be breaking up. It was cracking and twisting and moving up and down. The noise sounded like the earth bellowing in mighty pain."

These were the words of a young schoolmaster, Noah W. Cooper, on the night of August 31, 1886, the night of the great South Carolina earthquake. Noah had come to Cool Spring to teach a two-month session at Pineville School, between Conway and Aynor. Noah's description of the quake was published in *The Mullins Enterprise* in 1951, and again in the 1970 tricentennial edition of *The Independent Republic Quarterly*.

The state had experienced devastating earthquakes in 1697 and 1799, both centering near Charleston and spiraling out to the rest of the state. But the area was sparsely settled in both periods, and few people even remembered that such tales had been told by earlier generations.

The center of the 1886 quake again lay between the towns of Charleston and Summerville. That area suffered the greatest damage. However, the shocks were so severe that every county in the Low Country could have claimed to be the center. The earthquake of 1886 is included in the list of the most severe earthquakes in the world between 1750 and 1950.

In Cool Spring and elsewhere, the initial shock took everyone by surprise. It happened about ten p.m. Most people were already in bed, and ran out of their houses in their nightclothes. They heard a roar, like thunder under the ground, and the earth heaved and swayed. Dogs barked in confusion, animals howled, chickens clucked and ran wild; the sounds of the terrified animals mingled with the screams and wails from the people. The bright harvest moon cast eerie shadows of tilting and trembling trees and buildings over the macabre landscape.

Schoolmaster Cooper was immediately aware that they were in the throes of a violent earthquake. The people of the small rural community had other ideas. They knew it was the end of the world, Judgment Day. Their time of reckoning was at hand.

Tremor after tremor shook the ground, each time bringing cries, shrieks, and prayers. Families huddled together out in the open, away from houses and swaying trees. Mothers gathered their children close and held on for the end.

Noah Cooper was boarding with Mr. Mayberry Mishoe. Everyone was scared, but Mishoe's son Bill trembled and cried out of control. It didn't help that Bill's mother-in-law sat beside him in her rocking chair, telling him that the end of the world would surely come before daylight.

After trying to reassure Bill and the Mishoes, Noah went, stumbling and falling the whole way, to the little schoolhouse. There he found the yard full of frightened people. They cried and moaned that they would be "swallowed up." Noah went from one to another, comforting them, answering questions. Then he stepped up onto the schoolhouse porch to address the crowd. He told them about famous earthquakes in history, emphasizing the fact that it was usually in cities, not the country, where people were killed. He said deep cracks seldom appeared in sandy areas like the coastal counties.

While Noah spoke, one of the worst shocks hit, damaging the school and toppling the chimney. A nearby field rolled like waves of the ocean. Great old trees leaped off the ground and collapsed, their roots ripped out of the soil. The crowd cried out louder than ever. The shock passed and Noah finally got them quieted and dispersed.

The long, terrible night finally passed into morning light.

According to Noah's account, "The earthquake worked a righteous revolution in the habits of the people." Churches were crowded with anxious worshippers for weeks afterward. Wine making ceased, drinking declined, and "stump-hole" whiskey stills were destroyed. Many people turned over a new leaf and vowed to lead better lives.

Several days later news began to trickle in from Charleston and Florence. Railroads had twisted and buckled, and telegraph lines fallen. The rumor passed through that Charleston had been destroyed by the quake and a resulting tidal wave. Travelers on horseback dispelled that, saying that there had been death and destruction in Charleston and Georgetown, but both towns still stood.

The earthquake of 1886 was felt throughout South Carolina, as well as in thirty states and Canada. President Grover Cleveland sent messages of sympathy, along with shipments of food, tents, and other supplies. Queen Victoria of England sent offers of assistance. As news of the quake spread, messages and help flooded into South Carolina from all over the world.

The number of dead and injured varies with the source of information. A newspaper account from Columbia noted that sixty had died in Charleston, with $68 million in damages. The Seismic Monitoring Center near Charleston estimated the damage at $23 million. Some books number the deaths at ninety-two; this probably includes those killed in Charleston and other towns that reported. The shocks and tremors continued for a month, so no exact count was ever made of damages or deaths. Surveyors estimated property damage in Charleston, but no effort was made to put a value on the destruction in rural areas. It was the age-old custom of country people to help each other and take care of their own problems.

No one living at the time ever forgot the panic and confusion of those days. Paul Quattlebaum, honored leader of Conway, often mentioned that he was born in the year of "the great shake."

Even fifty years later, people dated the events of their lives as occurring before or after the great earthquake of 1886.

17

The *Freeda A. Wyley*

The Old Shipwreck

If you are lucky, you may see it.

Of course, that depends on a number of factors, such as the season of the year, high tides, hurricanes or northeasters, and the progress of the Grand Strand Beach Renourishment Program.

In years past the century-old shipwreck served as a dependable landmark near 43rd Avenue North in Myrtle Beach. It had its own historical marker and enough "native" residents to tell the story to newcomers. Now it lies covered by layer after layer of heavy sand, trucked in to repair tidal and storm damage. Some days you see little evidence that this stretch of beach is the final resting place of a proud trading ship, the *Freeda A. Wyley,* which wrecked and burned in the Great Storm of 1893. Other days, high tides and lashing waves steal sand and cause the wreck to rise, stark and bare.

The National Registry of ships listed the *Freeda A. Wyley* as a 507-ton barkentine, a three-masted vessel with a square-rigged fore-mast and two fore-and-aft rigged sails. This combination of sails had been used since the time of the Crusades to the Holy Land. The square sail gave greater speed and power at sea, while the fore-and-aft sails made tacking and steering easier. A few of the ships were used for coastal trade into the 1920s because of their reliability and economy.

The *Freeda A. Wyley,* out of Thomaston, Maine, was making a regular run between Pascagoula, Mississippi and New York City. It carried a cargo of fresh yellow pine lumber cut from virgin forests in the Deep South. Northern cities provided a steady market for pine lumber, so hundreds of ships were engaged in similar voyages.

Once the ships left Gulf ports they were out of touch with any news or weather reports. Their crews relied entirely on seamanship skills in all kinds of weather. Sailing around Florida, with its treacherous islands and keys, was the slowest part of the voyage. The South Atlantic coast had few good ports, so the ships stayed at sea unless they needed medical help or food and water.

As the ships pushed northward late in August, 1893, the crews took note of heavily overcast skies and rough seas. After they passed Savannah, the weather dramatically worsened. Late summer was the season for violent Atlantic storms. They hoped this storm would be no worse than others they had experienced and survived.

Along the coast of the Carolinas, barrier reefs and islands made navigating tricky, at best, so ships could not sail too close to land. As the fury of the storm increased, surging tides and high winds caught up walls of water that washed over the decks. Crews had no choice but to try to ride it out under bare masts, with a headsail or storm jig. The splintering of masts and loss of rigging left many ships drifting helplessly toward land. All the crews could do was pray.

The hurricane, later called "The Great Storm," reached its peak on the night of August 29th. Past midnight, a ship was reported burning like a torch north of Frying Pan Shoals, near the mouth of the Cape Fear River. No one knows what started the blaze. In such a storm it could have been an upset galley stove or overturned lantern.

The burning ship was identified as the *Freeda A. Wyley.* The schooner *Yamassee* managed to get close enough to see the ship's nameplate while it was still legible, and search for the crew. Evidently they had abandoned ship–their fate is still unknown.

The Captain's Log, tattered and weather damaged, was found later near Shallotte Point, North Carolina. The last entry, dated August 29, 1893, said simply, "Heaven help us."

The *Freeda A. Wyley* burned to the turn of her bilge keel. What was left, the bottom of the hull, drifted aimlessly at the mercy of tides and winter storms. She finally came in on an even keel, to find a resting place in the gentle crescent cove known as Long Bay, between Little River and Georgetown. Today, the burned skeleton of the old sailing vessel nestles deeper in the sand at Myrtle Beach, far from its home port in New England.

The remains of the *Freeda A. Wyley*

Estimates are that seventy northbound ships were lost in the storm, their wreckage and scattered cargoes littering the beaches from Hilton Head to Cape Hatteras. Salvage crews set to work immediately, leaving little to identify the ships. Many southbound ships capsized and sank, never to be traced, because of their lack of heavy cargo.

Lloyd's of London, which publishes shipping information daily, confirmed the loss of the *Freeda A. Wyley,* along with about a hundred other ships in the Great Storm of 1893. The hurricane caused two thousand deaths and over $10 million damage along the Atlantic coast.

The old shipwreck is the only one visible along the beach. Its historical marker is missing, but the *Freeda A. Wyley* is still worth looking for.

18

The *Jonathan May*

Of Ships and Salvage

The hurricane season runs from August through November. In 1893 there were two major hurricanes, and therefore it is called "a killer year of storms." The Great Storm in August which destroyed the *Freeda A. Wyley* was followed by another storm in October, with more violent winds and a tidal wave striking deep into Murrells Inlet. The loss of lives and property was catastrophic.

Less well known than the wreck of the *Freeda A. Wyley* is the story of another ship, the *Jonathan May*. The Great Storm of August, 1893 also wrecked and tossed the *May* ashore in the sheltered Long Bay Cove of the Grand Strand.

The *Jonathan May*, a three-masted schooner at 379 tons, was smaller than the *Wyley*. Captain George N. Cook sailed out of Philadelphia with a load of lumber for ports in the Deep South. Receiving no warning, the *Jonathan May* sailed directly into the path of the hurricane. Shipping lanes lie beyond barrier islands and offshore reefs, but the strong winds and high tides pushed the ships toward land. And toward their deaths.

The *Jonathan May* capsized near Frying Pan Shoals, close to Wilmington. The crew cut away masts and rigging before abandoning the ship and trying to save themselves on a raft. They held on as the seas tossed and tortured them. Days later, the suffering crew was

A barkentine vessel

rescued by the schooner *Ann E. Valentine* from New Brunswick, and finally taken back to their home port of Philadelphia.

Left to the mercy of the wind and tide, the *Jonathan May* came ashore later in Myrtle Beach. It drifted in south of Singleton Swash to lodge in the sand near 75th Avenue North.

The news spread instantly.

A treasure-trove of finished lumber lay on the sand, with the schooner on its side and abandoned by its crew. Its cargo was fair game for anyone who could reach the beach in time to get their share.

They came from near and far, determined men with wagons or drays pulled by mules or yoke of oxen. No regard was given to the owners of the ship and cargo. It was every man for himself, carrying away what he needed or could sell. The story goes that numerous fine homes along the coast and farther inland were built with the lumber. The hull of the schooner consisted of planking forty-four feet long and fourteen inches wide, under copper sheathing. Fine lumber has many uses.

What remained of the wreck of the ship lay on the beach, covered most of the time by sand. Hurricane Hazel struck in 1954 and tore the hull apart, scattering much of it over land and ocean. Some parts like the ship's rail survived nearly intact. Once again men came to salvage what they could, this time with trucks instead of wagon and oxen. A gift from the sea, they figured: seasoaked wood for rafters and mantels, porch railings and benches, and imaginative interior fittings.

Not all of the treasure could be pried from the sandy grave, and beachcombers have continued to unearth parts of the ship. In 1958 the great brass rudder was discovered, sixty-five years after the Great Storm. With blades twenty-six feet long from their post, the rudder was found by a young boy digging in the sand. He must have thought he had struck riches beyond belief.

Battered fragments of the wreck have been picked up and burned in fireplaces, glowing in rainbow colors of purple, yellow, green, and blue, another gift from the restless ocean.

After Hurricane Hugo in 1989, the old ship's final resting place couldn't be found. The *Jonathan May* has vanished, and become just another statistic. Another shipwreck legend.

The train enters Myrtle Beach in the early 1900s
Reprinted from the Anchor Bank Collection of Home-Town Classics

19

The Black Maria

Everyone called her the "Black Maria." The black mass of the old wood-burning engine and the huge clouds of smoke, grime, and cinders all made the name stick. No matter what the size or shape or color, she was a welcome sight to the little lumber camp settlement of New Town (Myrtle Beach). The railroad formed a desperately needed link with the outside world in 1900.

The Black Maria was the first locomotive used on the newly constructed line, The Conway Coast and Western Railroad. The tracks began east of the Waccamaw River at Conway and ran straight to Pine Island, a huge lumber mill near the present site of Waccamaw Pottery. The tracks then curved and proceeded to the beach, extending along Ninth Avenue into what is now the Myrtle Beach Pavilion parking lot, ending at a small wooden depot.

Everyone watched the progress of the lines being laid. A news item in the *Horry Herald* in September, 1899 stated: "The seacoast railroad is growing longer every day and shortening the distance between its terminus and the beach. It has reached a point about eight miles from the beach, leaving four or five miles to be completed, which will be done by the next season."

The Black Maria came from a logging camp near Pireway, just over the North Carolina line. There she ran on a tram road of wooden rails, pulling logs out of the swamp. When that logging camp was abandoned, teams of oxen hauled the engine to Whiteville, North Carolina, and on to the railroad at Chadburn. By December, 1887 the Chadburn line had extended to Conway, where the tracks ran down the dirt road called Main Street.

The railroad tracks reached Pine Island in 1900. From Conway, the Black Maria and its cars had to be ferried across the Waccamaw River. The railroad drawbridge wasn't built until 1904, so the train's regular run was to the beach and back to the river.

The development of the railroad to Myrtle Beach was the dream and accomplishment of the Burroughs family of Conway. F. G. Burroughs and his son, F. A. Burroughs, surveyed the route in 1896. While the tracks were being laid, the Burroughs and Collins Company built the three-story Seaside Inn, which opened in 1901. They also built a general store, the company commissary, and cleared bushes and trees from a few sandy streets near the hotel.

Traveling by train was an exciting sign of progress for the Grand Strand in the emerging new century, although not one without risk. Sparks from smokestacks often set the woods afire near the tracks. When that happened the engineer stopped the train, the crew beat out the fire, and then they continued on their way. Other hazards were the cattle and hogs that roamed freely through the countryside. Frightened at first by the noise and smoke, the animals sometimes stampeded as the train approached. The razorback hogs, also called "piney woods rooters," took off for the cover of thick bushes. The cows soon grew used to the noise and confusion, and sometimes lay down on the soft warm sand at grade crossings. The engineer would have to stop the train to run them off the tracks. "Cowcatchers" were well-named and necessary. The railroad company had to pay six dollars a head for animals killed on the tracks.

Late in 1900, a huge whale washed ashore near Hurl Rocks, and the news spread rapidly throughout Horry County. Everyone wanted to see the whale; excursion trains came from Conway. The company fitted flat cars with cross ties and boards laid across for seats. The tracks extended to Pine Island, so the crowds of people had to walk the rest of the way to the beach. A few wagons met the trains. Some people brought picnic baskets. A party of whalers showed up to strip the blubber and meat from the carcass. The harpooned whale had gotten away from them in a storm. They left the whale's skeleton on the beach, and children played on it until it was towed away.

People were used to riding wagons and buggies, bouncing along deeply rutted, sandy roads, fording streams and creeks, and then having to wait for the river ferry. Riding the train felt like riding the wind, a great adventure as they hurtled along at twenty-five or thirty miles per hour.

By 1904 the railroad extended from Conway to Aynor, by way of Cool Spring, another small community. Families now came from all over the region to vacation at the beach.

The Black Maria served the Myrtle Beach line four years before it was replaced by coal-burning locomotives. The train delivered food, mail, produce, supplies, and ice, the most popular item in the summer. When necessary, the train made an extra run to Conway to get medicine or to take someone to the doctor.

In 1912 the Atlantic Coastline Railroad bought the line and operated it profitably for decades. The faithful old wood-burner, the Black Maria, was sold to a lumber company at Enterprise Landing, near Socastee, and used again for logging. It was finally abandoned in the woods near the landing, where it still sits, rusting, with trees and bushes growing up through it. It is a symbol of another era.

Myrtle Beach at the turn of the century
Photograph by Dr. C. J. Epps
Reprinted from the Anchor Bank Collection of Home-Town Classics

20

Vacationing in 1902

Myrtle Beach in the Early Years

People came to the South Carolina shore in the late 1800s to enjoy fishing, crabbing, shrimping, and the beach. Hard working farmers sometimes pitched tents and camped a few days in the fall, after the crops were harvested. Around the turn of the century a few families from Conway and Bucksport began to build cottages, little more than rough shelters, to make their stay more enjoyable. And the development of the beach began.

The few vacationers who came to the Grand Strand found golden sun, clear blue water, breathtaking sunrises, and gorgeous moons for courting couples to stroll under on the beach. The pure white sand, unpolluted and unmarred, stretched five hundred feet wide at low tide. The high sand dunes, with their natural covering of sea oats and wild grasses, marked the edge of the high water mark. Early visitors who had never seen the beach marveled at the beauty.

This wonderland was New Town, or Myrtle Beach, about 1902.

The dozen or so children of summer visitors ran and played on the beach from morning until night. They paddled and swam in the shallow water, caught crabs and sand fiddlers, and looked for perfect shells and sand dollars. There was a mysterious old burned shipwreck about two miles up the beach. Or they could climb on Hurl Rocks.

In the afternoons, the children liked to meet the fishing boats coming in, so they could see the catch or buy fish for supper. A string of a dozen large fish cost one shiny quarter.

The children took showers by throwing buckets of cold water on each other, then ran to meet the slow-moving train from Conway. With its wood-burning engine called the "Black Maria," the train brought mail, supplies, and the fathers of summer families from their jobs in town. One man sent his cow over on the train so the children could have milk.

The boys and girls often slipped out to the sand dunes after supper, in the long summer twilight, to gaze at the stars and swap ghost stories. The dogs went with them, while the adults sat and rocked on the porches. Sometimes the children were interrupted by great grunting monsters; then they screamed and ran back to the safety of the porches. The dogs ran too, smart enough to stay out of the monsters' way. The beasts were razorback hogs and cattle from the woods and farms farther inland, toward Socastee. With no stock law to confine them, the animals roamed freely, searching for food. They were the first garbage collectors at the beach. The worst thing the hogs did was root under the houses at night and keep people awake. Cows and goats kept the grass cropped right down to the dunes. They sometimes climbed over the dunes and stood in shallow water to escape the pesky flies.

The few summer cottages were scattered along Ninth Avenue and Chester Street, from the Kings Highway to the pavilion area. The houses were built simply, with rough, unpainted weatherboard nailed outside and no inside wall board or paneling. They perched precariously close to the sand dunes and served as cool, airy shelters from the sun and rain.

Everyone accepted sand, grit, and dust as part of beach-living. It was fun to feel that you were camping or roughing it on vacation. People made light of hardships, but there were many.

There was no electricity or refrigeration. Lighting depended on candles or oil lamps that always smoked in sudden gusts of wind. Cooking had to be done on a wood stove in a back room, as early in the day as possible due to the heat. Each house had a well or hand pump, or shared one with a neighbor, and each had an outhouse. The Conway Ice Company sent blocks of ice packed in sawdust on the train to the beach. Summer visitors bought as many blocks as they could get.

An item in the *Horry Herald* for August 8, 1900 read: "The name of the seashore terminus of the Conway and Seashore Railroad has been changed from New Town to Myrtle Beach." The limited use of the train made a difference in the number of people coming to the beach. Another item in the *Horry Herald* on May 23, 1901 noted: "The season at Myrtle Beach will open in a short time now, and the Seaside Inn will be open to the public (for the first time), with Mr. F. A. Burroughs as proprietor and Mr. C. H. Snider as manager."

It was the first hotel and the first official tourist season for Myrtle Beach. The big new hotel had no electricity or indoor plumbing. The price: two dollars a day for a room and three meals.

Also in 1901 the post office moved from Withers Swash, about two miles south, to the company store near the pavilion. The name changed from Withers to Myrtle Beach.

The inn, pavilion, commissary (store), depot, and railroad were all built by the Burroughs and Collins Company of Conway, to develop the beach and its lumber interests. The pine forests had provided the region with its oldest industries. Sap was used to produce tar, pitch, and turpentine. By 1890 lumber became a more important money-maker in South Carolina. The Burroughs and

The pine forests attracted early industries and settlements.
Top: Barrels of turpentine produced from "scraping a pine tree."
Bottom: Loggers at the turn of the century produced lumber for
export and the building along the beach.
Photos courtesy of the Horry County Museum

Collins mill at Pine Island, about four miles inland, sawed lumber for the beach buildings.

A board walk connected the Seaside Inn to the pavilion, an octagonal gray building with a red roof and wide open windows. A Delco system later furnished electricity for both structures.

The center of night life on the beach was the pavilion. An old wind-up Victrola and a dozen scratchy records provided dance music. The older people sat on the wide porch and rocked, watching the dancers and the children. If anyone could play a guitar or a fiddle, they were persuaded to provide live entertainment. Boys sold lemonade, candy, and peanuts. On Sundays, worship services were sometimes held in the pavilion.

A dirt road ran from Conway to Socastee, and in 1914 it was extended to the beach. It was a twenty-one mile, winding, sandy, wagon track, but more summer visitors came. Yet, by 1915, only seven families lived at the beach year-round. They worked for the company.

Summer cottages weren't suitable for winter weather. Winters were mild, but they could be damp with near freezing temperatures. "Nor'easters" brought gale-force winds and high tides. Burroughs and Collins Company built a few houses, sturdier and more permanent, for the lumber camp workers. As winter winds lashed the beaches and swept over the dunes, fireplaces heated the houses. Piles of stacked wood stood in every yard.

During the winter months, the beach looked bleak and deserted. But changes came quickly. The train brought more and more summer visitors. A few people bought lots to build houses. Ocean-front lots sold for $25. If you bought a lot and built a house worth $500, you got another lot free.

Would you consider a deal like that?

The growth and development of Myrtle Beach and the Grand Strand into today's resort went slowly. Simeon B. Chapin saw the need for the Chapin Department Store in 1927, the oldest store along the Grand Strand. Chapin, a well-known financier and philanthropist from New York and Chicago, was a founding partner of Myrtle Beach Farms Company (now Burroughs and Chapin Company), which played a major role in the early beach development. Chapin's generosity led to Chapin Memorial Library, Chapin Memorial Park, Chapin Foundation of South Carolina, and contributions to a host of other causes. Roberta McMillan made the Blue Sea Inn a popular site for tourists and locals in the 1930s and 40s. She introduced the first efficiency apartments on the beach during World War II. Her husband, Robert, brought the first merry-go-round to the Pavilion Amusement Park. These and other pioneers started the building of the Grand Strand, but most of the growth came in the last thirty years.

Even in 1902, vacations here were something special.

The Seaside Inn soon after it opened
Courtesy of the Horry County Museum

21

The First School on the Grand Strand

"Watch out for Bears!"

In the early 1900s, getting an education on the Grand Strand was difficult. There was the two-room Pine Island School near Socastee, but it was an arduous trip for children from the beach. By 1915 a school had been built closer to the lumber camp settlement called Myrtle Beach, providing for children who lived there year-round.

The school was located where Third Avenue North comes into West Broadway (the Old Conway Highway), near LaZelle's Flower Shop. The building was set back from the narrow, sandy street. Several huge oak trees shaded the play area in front. Clarence Macklin's store stood on the corner near the street, a source of candy for anyone lucky enough to have pennies. Near the trees, an artesian well flowed freely with water for the school and homes close by. Two small outhouses near Withers Ditch served as toilet facilities.

The one-story, white clapboard building had narrow brick chimney flues for the wood-burning stoves that heated the rooms. Small brick pillows supported the building, which was open underneath. Sometimes pets waited under the building for children to come out and play. Often wild hogs rooted and snorted under the school until someone scared them away.

The school's two large rooms could be divided by folding doors to make four classrooms, in which ten grades were taught. With several grades in a classroom, children worked quietly until it was their turn to recite. Many times children skipped grades because they had already learned the material by listening carefully.

One room held a small stage, used every Friday for plays and programs. All the classes planned programs for special occasions, with parents attending, and the children singing or "speaking pieces." The room was also used by the community for meetings and revivals.

Walking to school was scary and even dangerous. Black bears roamed freely through the river swamps and bays, and were often seen in the pine and yaupon thickets that lined the path to the school. Usually an adult armed with a club walked with the children. Sometimes they took the dogs, and always they were warned, "Be careful, and watch out for bears!"

School days were long. Lunch recess gave time to sit with friends on the big roots under the oaks, eat lunches, and then play games: hide-and-seek, bat ball, drop the handkerchief, follow the leader, "Red Rover come over," or boys chase the girls (the favorite). Recess was the high point of the day.

In 1928 the state constructed a brick building, with electricity and indoor plumbing, which housed elementary and high school classes until it burned in 1946.

The site of the first little school on West Broadway is now a vacant lot. Hogs no longer snort there, and bears no longer wander over the grounds. The happy sounds of children have gone, but if you listen with your heart, you may hear them still.

22

The Ocean Forest Hotel
"The Grand Old Lady"

The children piled out of their daddy's Model T Ford. They stood in the sand and stared, speechless, for once. Never had they seen such a sight.

"Is it a magic castle?" one of them whispered.

The Ocean Forest Hotel, rising ten stories above its backdrop of wide, blue Atlantic Ocean, surely looked like a magic castle to children during the years of the Great Depression. A hotel in Myrtle Beach that cost a million dollars to build–and it had real elevators.

In the 1920s Holmes B. Springs was vice-president of Woodside National Bank in Greenville, South Carolina. Springs had accompanied General John J. Pershing in 1916-17 during his pursuit of the Mexican bandit Pancho Villa, and then again when Pershing led the American Expeditionary Force in World War I. Springs was decorated for meritorious war service. Colonel Springs' strong belief in the potential growth and development of the Grand Strand led him to encourage the four Woodside brothers to invest in the beach. Myrtle Beach Farms Company wanted to sell 66,000 acres of undeveloped land north of the little village. John T. Woodside, wealthy industrialist and banker, and his three brothers bought this property in 1926. Its development became their dream.

They envisioned a majestic hotel as the centerpiece, surrounded by winding avenues, homes, fresh water lakes, stables and riding trails, golf courses, and scenic forests. All this, of course, fronted by the unspoiled beach. For the resort they chose the name "Arcady," a form of the ancient Greek word *Arkadia,* a place of unbelievable peace and beauty. The resort would be dedicated to luxury and pleasure on an international scale.

The Woodsides chose Raymond Hood, a Rhode Island architect, to design the complex of buildings, and named A. A. Ainsworth of New York as chairman of Arcady Executives, Inc.

In 1926 the lumbering and fishing village of Myrtle Beach had one store and less than two hundred residents. The locals watched the building begin, scarcely believing what they saw. The state and nation watched as well. Everyone predicted the magnificent structure would rival those in New York, Miami, the French Riviera, or any other vacation spot for the rich and famous.

As the building progressed, armies of decorators arrived, sparing no detail for comfort, luxury, and beauty. Fresh and salt water were piped to the rooms. Doormen, waitresses, and maids wore uniforms to match the decor. The high-ceilinged ballrooms and dining rooms featured imported crystal chandeliers and Italian marble frieze work and columns. Meeting rooms, reception rooms, an arcade of fine shops, art gallery, and several dining rooms would meet the needs of convention groups. Young people could enjoy the indoor and outdoor swimming pools, game rooms, and terraces for dancing under the stars to Big Bands like Guy Lombardo's.

The ten-story center tower, flanked on each side by a five-story section with balconies and terraces, stood gleaming white against the blue ocean and green native trees and shrubbery. The steel and concrete building was considered totally fireproof. With more than three hundred rooms, including 220 elaborately appointed guest rooms, the hotel ranked as one of the largest buildings in the United States.

The Ocean Forest Hotel's grand opening celebration was February 21, 1930. Unfortunately, the stock market had crashed a few months earlier in October, 1929.

The Ocean Forest Hotel
Courtesy of the Horry County Museum

The crash caused the loss of fortunes and dreams for thousands, including the Woodsides. The completed parts of their plan, the hotel and country club across the highway, changed hands and continued to operate. During the Depression years of the 1930s, people still came to vacation or honeymoon in the hotel, despite a persistent rumor that an illegal gambling casino in the tower rooms attracted shady and dangerous visitors from faraway places. The economy improved after World War II, and convention groups found the hotel perfect for their needs.

In 1954 Hurricane Hazel damaged or destroyed most new motels, but the "Grand Old Lady" stood intact and unharmed. The hotel enjoyed mild success in the 1960s, but new motels offered stiff competition with affordable family rates. As the hotel changed hands, repairs were often overlooked. The Grand Old Lady grew shabby and seedy in her old age, and closed in June, 1974. The owners decided the land was more valuable than the building and made plans to demolish it. Some people opposed the plan and tried to save the hotel, but the owners went ahead.

On Friday, the thirteenth of September, 1974, the Ocean Forest Hotel imploded and crashed to the ground. What once had been a child's magic castle, was carted off as debris.

23

The Whiskey Ship

An unusual event took place along the Grand Strand in 1930 or 1931. No one can verify the exact date. The Eighteenth Amendment prohibited the manufacture and sale of alcoholic beverages of any kind throughout the United States. To enforce the federal law, the Volstead Act and the Jones Law were passed by congress, defining alcoholic drinks and providing fines up to $10,000 for violations, plus five years in prison.

The Women's Christian Temperance Union celebrated the Prohibition Amendment. Just about everyone else in Horry County despised it. For the most part, the new law was simply ignored, especially by people who brewed their own wine, corn "likker," or stump-hole whiskey.

When someone didn't show for the country store meetings, the word went around: "He got caught!" No one asked questions. They understood. They also enthusiastically welcomed back those that had to serve time.

The coastline of the United States attracted smugglers and blockade runners. Coves and inlets provided some protection, but the vigilant coastal patrol arrested large numbers of smugglers. Still the illegal trade continued. There were just too many customers who would pay for imported alcoholic beverages.

On a moonless, stormy night in late summer of 1930 (or 1931), a regular "run" took place. A small, swift ship, loaded with the finest imported wines and whiskey, hovered offshore waiting for the all-clear signal. The ship planned to come in to the Second Avenue Fishing Pier, quickly unload the contraband, and make a quick getaway. The hour was late. In the tiny village of Myrtle Beach no one was around to observe the activities about to take place.

When the signal came, the action began. Except something went wrong. Either the high tide or the wind pushed the ship too far inland, or maybe the boat's skipper wasn't familiar with the coast. At any rate, the ship ran solidly aground on a sandbar. There was no hope of sailing free. The crew knew well the fines and prison terms for (a) smuggling, (b) rum-running, (c) illegal trade in an unlawful substance. Finding themselves in trouble, they knew just what to do. They abandoned ship.

The crew thought there had been no observers in Myrtle Beach, but people came to that grounded ship as if flares had been lit. They approached quietly, eager to get their share of the contraband. Small boats ferried cases and bottles to shore, where the haul was divided. People carted away as much as they could carry.

When dawn came, the ship sat lodged on the sandbar, with no crew on board. And no cargo. Authorities investigated and asked questions, but received few answers. Later the coastal patrol came and towed the empty boat away.

Along the Grand Strand, no one discussed the event. Everyone had been sound asleep that night. No one had any idea of what had happened. Although they occasionally admitted to hearing tales of quart jars being used, and whiskey bottles smashed or buried to eliminate the evidence. Other stories told of ornate whiskey bottles still around, more than sixty years later, as a memento of the event. But no one tells the names of the participants, even to this day.

The 2nd Avenue Fishing Pier

A Survey History of Horry County, The Independent Republic mentions that the economy of Little River was helped by smuggling of alcoholic beverages during the Prohibition Era. Fishing boats met other boats at sea, carrying on illegal trade. The same was true of other small ports. The contraband found its way up and down the coast to illegal "speakeasies," casinos, and nightclubs. The finest quality alcoholic beverages were brought in from the Bahamas and Cuba.

National Prohibition, the 18th Amendment, was repealed by the 21st Amendment to the Constitution, ratified in December, 1933.

More people celebrated that one.

The Atalaya tower, located in the central palm court

24

Atalaya

Castle in the Sand

It was his childhood dream come true, his Spanish "Castle in the Sand."

Arthur Milton Huntington traveled extensively with his parents in Europe. He admired Moorish fortresses on the southern coast of Spain, built with low, sturdy walls to withstand the onslaught of Atlantic storms. Much later, he adapted the plan and design to fit the location he chose for a winter home on the sometimes stormy coast of South Carolina. Atalaya was one of several homes owned by Huntington and his wife, Anna Hyatt Huntington, a renowned sculptress. Atalaya means "watchtower."

Since the early 1930s, Huntington's Castle in the Sand has stood among palm trees and native myrtles and pines, firmly anchored in deep sand near the beach. The unusual building is located in Huntington State Park, known from Colonial days as Magnolia Beach. The 2,500-acre park lies about three miles south of Murrells Inlet, across the King's Highway from the entrance to Brookgreen Gardens. A private estate until Huntington's death in 1955, it became a state park in 1960. The area has remained a natural habitat for salt water and fresh water wildlife like alligators and birds. Convenient boardwalks help interested viewers.

Huntington inherited a vast fortune from his father, Collis P.

Huntington, railroad and steamship magnate and one of the richest men in the world. In 1930 the Huntingtons bought four adjoining plantations: Brookgreen, The Oaks, Laurel Hill, and Springfield. The land stretched from the Waccamaw River to the Atlantic Ocean. They planned outdoor statuary gardens to display the work of Mrs. Huntington and other sculptors. Today the magnificent gardens rank among the very finest anywhere in the world.

For their private estate and home, the Huntingtons chose the beach side of their nine thousand acres. Mrs. Huntington was tubercular most of her life. They hoped the warm moist climate and clean ocean breezes would help her. The planning and building of Atalaya took place between 1930 and 1934, the darkest days of the Great Depression. Huntington's great fortune had remained intact, but he realized how many Americans were jobless, homeless, and destitute. He hired local people to work for him, both in the gardens and in building his home. He offered jobs and learning opportunities to local brick masons, their helpers, carpenters, painters, craftsmen of all kinds, gardeners, and landscapers. The millions of dollars Huntington spent benefited the local economy at the time it most needed help.

Like the old Spanish fortresses, the castle nestles low in the sand, surrounding a large open courtyard with covered walkways leading to a forty-foot-high central tower. Tall palm trees, creeping fig, and shrubbery offer relief from the hot summer sun. The building stretches two hundred feet on each side, with brick stairways to the roof and to underground storage rooms, curving brick walls and archways, and patterned brick floors. Since the castle was heated entirely by open fireplaces, the thirty-six rooms contain twenty-two fireplaces. Huntington wanted to give the brick masons work, and he wanted a fireproof building.

He had steel beams run through the outer walls, reinforcing them in case of earthquakes or violent coastal storms. The windows are protected by iron grillwork designed by Mrs. Huntington. The castle has withstood two major hurricanes and several other "hard blows" with minor damage.

The castle plan included a spacious studio where Anna Hyatt Huntington created some of her most popular pieces. Located on the end of the south wing, the studio featured a high ceiling with a twenty-five-foot skylight, a massive fireplace, and a smaller courtyard with horse stables, dog kennels, and bear cages for her authentic models. For one piece of sculpture, Mrs. Huntington imported deerhounds from Scotland.

Because the rooms were so spread out around the central quadrangle, Huntington installed a house telephone system. Mrs. Huntington could call for a cup of tea or sandwich at any time and continue with her work.

For their brief stays at Atalaya, the Huntingtons installed beautiful furnishings and carpets. They entertained countless guests, who eagerly explored the unique castle. Oysters were in such demand for them and their guests that they set aside a special "oyster-shucking" room. After Huntington's death, the furnishings were moved to other homes. Anna Hyatt Huntington died in 1973 at the age of ninety-eight.

Atalaya is open to the public. It hosts in the fall months special arts and crafts shows. These are juried shows, with artists and artisans coming from all over the Southeast. Thousands come for the day, to see and buy unusual artwork. Yet the main attraction is the castle itself, with its amazing brickwork and rooms–Archer Huntington's Castle in the Sand.

"Fighting Stallions"
by Anna Hyatt Huntington

25

Brookgreen Gardens

Brookgreen Gardens, characterized as "Another World" for its timeless beauty, had its beginning in 1931. The anniversary of this date is celebrated each July with a giant birthday party, held on the lawn near the visitor's pavilion. The party is open to the public, and includes special entertainment and refreshments.

Founded by Archer Milton Huntington and his wife, sculptress Anna Hyatt Huntington, the unique garden museum contains the world's largest exhibit of American figurative sculpture. Originally planned as a showcase for Mrs. Huntington's work, the gardens now have 547 pieces on display, created by 241 artists. Sixty-eight statues were sculpted by Mrs. Huntington.

In 1929 the Huntingtons sailed from New York City on their yacht for a leisurely trip to the West Indies. A stop in Georgetown for supplies included some sightseeing. Riding north along Waccamaw Neck, they saw several plantations for sale. They returned in January, 1930 and purchased four adjoining properties: The Oaks, Brookgreen, Springfield, and Laurel Hill.

The plantations were so isolated they could scarcely be reached except by the Waccamaw River. The King's Highway was still a sandy, rutted wagon track, ending at the ferry across the Waccamaw into Georgetown.

The Huntingtons viewed their Low Country acreage, with its

native trees and plants, and a great avenue of 250-year-old oaks, as a fine natural setting for sculpture. Near the kitchen of the burned house at Brookgreen, they discovered a neglected formal boxwood garden, just waiting to be restored.

Materials for building their home, Atalaya, as well as the walkways and walls in the gardens, had to be brought in by boats along the river. Skilled local workers followed the plans created by the Huntingtons and talented landscaper, Frank G. Tarbox, Jr. They achieved a gracious and beautiful setting.

Mrs. Huntington created most of her best-known sculpture in her large studio at Atalaya. For years boats delivered her supplies. She used animals as live models. Mrs. Huntington created "Fighting Stallions," which stands at the garden entrance, at the suggestion of her husband. The sculpture is fifteen feet high, and ranks as one of the largest aluminum castings on record.

The gardens have grown and expanded over the years, with new areas opened for statuary and preservation of natural surroundings and wildlife. First class public facilities help attract families, school classes, tour groups, and visiting celebrities.

In 1992 Brookgreen Gardens, including Atalaya, was named a National Historic Landmark, one of two thousand sites so honored. Contributing culture and beauty, the gardens add to the special lure of the Grand Strand.

26

Myrtle Beach State Park

In 1933 the area now known as Myrtle Beach State Park was a virgin forest of native pine, cedar, oak, yaupon, holly, and wax myrtle. The dense undergrowth was practically impenetrable. Small animals and numerous species of birds claimed it as their sanctuary.

The inauguration of President Franklin Delano Roosevelt in 1933 brought "New Deal" policies, aimed at helping a nation devastated by the Great Depression. In 1934 the South Carolina State Park System purchased 312 acres of land to establish a park along the Grand Strand. The project was part of the Works Progress Administration (WPA).

The WPA, in cooperation with the Forestry Commission, decided to preserve the coastal landscape and native vegetation while creating a recreation facility. The work went fast because of the Civilian Conservation Corps workers, young men willing to do hard manual labor for small pay. These young men came from their Conway camp. They cleared roads, hiking trails, camp sites, and picnic areas. They built picnic shelters and a boardwalk along the beach, more shelters farther inland, five cabins for campers, a bath house and pavilion, and several coquina walks. The young men enjoyed the cool ocean breezes and promise of a quick swim after their day's work.

The park opened in 1935. The beautiful two-story pavilion stood on a high sand hill overlooking the ocean. From a distance it looked like an ante-bellum plantation home. The spacious upstairs room could be used for group meetings or assemblies, with park offices and bath house located on the ground level.

Large crowds had already used the park before its official opening date of June 1, 1937. The opening ceremony attracted local and state leaders. It marked a new era of more emphasis on tourism and recreation.

The park was turned over in 1942 to Myrtle Beach Army Air Base (across the King's Highway) for the recreation of the soldiers and German prisoners of war. The park reopened to the public after World War II.

In 1950 Springs Mills Foundation of Lancaster, South Carolina built the first fishing pier for the park as a gift to the state. The fine pier collapsed during Hurricane Hazel in October, 1954. It was rebuilt in 1956. When Myrtle Beach Air Force Base was reactivated in 1956, the 642-foot pier lay directly in the runway flight pattern. Two planes crashed because of this. Workers dismantled the pier and moved it a half mile south, where the seven hundred-foot pier still stands.

The Springs Mills Foundation again helped the park in 1957 with the magnificent gift of an Olympic-sized swimming pool, located in front of the pavilion. The beautiful pavilion had to be removed in the 1960s because of dampness, dry rot, and termites. The bath house was enlarged and modernized.

Today the park offers visitors fishing from the beach or the pier, swimming, convenient bath houses, well-marked hiking trails, picnic shelters and cookout facilities, daily nature study, and recreational programs for all ages. The 350 camp sites are used year-round, with the fall and spring months almost as popular as summer. There are waiting lists for reservations.

In 1963 an estimated 900,000 visitors used the park. In 1993 more than nine million visitors used it. A new entrance south of the old one on King's Highway now welcomes all who come.

There are forty-seven state parks in South Carolina; the most popular one is at Myrtle Beach.

27

The Intracoastal Waterway

President George Washington, a skilled surveyor, saw the value of connecting tidal streams, rivers, and bays for protection of commercial traffic. He suggested plans for a navigable canal in the Great Dismal Swamp area of North Carolina and Virginia. Coastal states needed canals to connect rivers.

In 1927 Congress finally authorized the building of the Intracoastal Waterway. The project was planned, supervised, and constructed by the U. S. Army Corps of Engineers. The plan was to take advantage of existing waterways to secure the shortest and most direct course.

The creation of the Inland Waterway Commission in 1931 got the work underway. The local commission body had the power to condemn property and acquire titles of needed lands and transfer them to the Corps of Engineers. By 1932 the preliminary work had been completed and hydraulic dredges were on the job.

The Great Depression was then at its worst in the South. Men came from far and wide to work a few weeks or longer. Some of them saw the Grand Strand as a new land of opportunity, and stayed. In 1935 Myrtle Beach had five hundred year-round residents. By 1938 the count was 1,200; the waterway construction was cited as the main reason for the growth.

Beginning with Little River, the Corps chose a straight passage to Socastee Creek and the Waccamaw River at Enterprise Landing. The twenty-three-mile section south of Little River passed through high areas, thirty feet or more in elevation. The workers cut, blasted, and drilled through coquina rock formations. The expensive and difficult work slowed the completion date for the entire project.

Temporary bridges had to be built at Nixon's Crossroads (North Myrtle Beach), Pine Island highway and railroad bridge at Myrtle Beach, and at Socastee. These kept highway traffic moving while the waterway was completed. Three drawbridges eventually replaced the temporary structures.

By November, 1935 the black Waccamaw River waters flowed into and blended with the clearer waters of Little River and various creeks and swamps. This joining near Socastee was the last part of the three thousand-mile waterway to be completed. A festive dedication ceremony was scheduled to take place at Socastee bridge on April 11, 1936.

Colonel Holmes B. Springs of Myrtle Beach, chairman of the Dedication Celebration Committee, presided over the historic event. Dignitaries from all over the country attended. The 17th Field Artillery Band from Fort Bragg provided the music. The ribbon cutting formally opened the last link of the Intracoastal Waterway. An ancient dream had come true.

Planners realized the waterway meant a passage for shipping that was safe from the threat of submarines, although they didn't believe a war would really come to our shores. It did five years later.

Today the waterway is the scene of boating, fishing, swimming, and water skiing. Pulpwood barges and other commercial craft pass north and south.

From Little River to Socastee, the waterway runs more or less parallel to Highway 17, until it becomes part of the Waccamaw River.

The only entrances are at Little River and Winyah Bay. Boaters marvel at the beauty of the Waccamaw River section, with moss-draped trees and plants along the banks. North of Socastee, the Pine Island Cut shows erosion of the tall cliff-like banks, laying bare the rock strata, tree roots, shells, fossils, and Indian artifacts. The waterway is peaceful and scenic, settling into the landscape, seemingly much older than its sixty years.

The U. S. Army Corps of Engineers and the U. S. Coast Guard share operation and maintenance of the waterway. They constantly check the depth of the channel, the navigational markers, and watch for landslides along the banks.

Along "Restaurant Row" and Barefoot Traders, several businesses claim a view of the waterway. Marinas offer sight-seeing tours south to the Waccamaw and Georgetown. Some choose to sail around Cherry Grove Point, through Hog Inlet into the Atlantic Ocean.

As a surveyor, George Washington knew what he was talking about.

28

The Civilian Conservation Corps

The "C Boys"

October 2, 1993 marked the end of an era: the Forestry Service closed their fire towers. These slender giants had stood as a sort of memorial to the work of the Civilian Conservation Corps in the 1930s. The "C-Boys" built four fire towers in Horry County: Meade Tower in East Conway on the Socastee Road, and towers near Aynor, Loris, and Wampee. Since then every boy and girl has dreamed of climbing the outside steps to the top.

The CCC camp near Conway was located along Highway 905 at Glass Hill. Built in 1934, the camp housed two hundred young men assigned to work in Horry County. The newcomers, uniformed and handsome, strong and healthy from hard work, attracted attention. Car loads of teenage girls rode by the camp and waved. Ministers invited the men to attend church. The C-Boys lived in barracks, under strict military rules, so they accepted opportunities to get out and meet local people. Many of them married and settled along the Grand Strand.

The CCC was one of the emergency programs set up in 1933 by Congress. Thanks to the Great Depression, young men had little hope of finding jobs. By joining the CCC, they earned thirty dollars a month. Twenty-two dollars of this was withheld and sent home to their families. That tiny amount saved scores of family farms, bought food and shoes for young children, and became the most important money many of those fresh-faced boys would ever earn.

Besides the small income, the CCC provided employment, instruction, a place to stay, uniforms to wear, and nourishing food. The young men received basic training that served them well later in the armed forces. More than two million men enlisted in the CCC between 1934 and 1942, when the program was discontinued because of World War II. The success of the Corps was due to excellent planning, advice from military leaders, and the organizational skills of General George C. Marshall.

Thirty CCC camps were scattered across South Carolina. The old camp on the Lumber River near Nichols looks like primitive log cabins, but the men were accustomed to hard work and outdoor life. Most of them had never had central heat, indoor plumbing, or air conditioning.

The State Parks System across the nation got its start from the work of the C-Boys. They cleared undergrowth, drained swamps, made trails and walks, built picnic shelters and cabins, and laid out park sites. They landscaped, planted grass, shrubbery, and trees, and worked to stop erosion. South Carolina enjoys forty-seven state parks set up by the Corps.

One thing the CCC gave us is kudzu. Imported from China and Japan, the vine was hailed as a quick beautification plant. It would grow anywhere and cover anything, even the devastation of strip mining or deep erosion. So the C-Boys planted kudzu and it grew, and grew, and grew. And it's still growing.

If we forgive the kudzu, the Civilian Conservation Corps served the nation well, with little publicity or recognition. Whether they were fighting fires or floods, clearing wooded areas or planting trees, constructing dams and bridges or re-routing streams, the C-Boys were on the job.

29

World War II

For adults, teenagers, and children, World War II marked the end of a way of life.

In December, 1941 the attack on Pearl Harbor brought the shocking realization that the American continent, with its apparent safety and isolation, was vulnerable to attack or retaliation. It wasn't a reassuring thought.

To people along the coast in Myrtle Beach, the war was an ever-present reality. The building of the Army Air Base in 1941 brought an influx of people and uniforms. It also brought the noise of planes overhead and the knowledge that their war games were practice for the real thing.

Rationing affected everyone, but this inconvenience evoked a feeling of pride, of tightening one's belt, of doing your part for your country and the armed forces. The same spirit of pride prompted attempts to grow vegetables by inept gardeners who wanted to join in the conversations about "victory gardens."

Another inconvenience was the blackout along the beaches and even farther inland. The plan included painting the upper half of car headlights black, using only the low beams, and never turning the lights directly toward the ocean. Civil Defense Units, made up of local volunteers, patrolled the beach.

Anyone who wondered why these precautions were necessary

just needed to take a walk along the beach at night. The sudden flares out on the horizon beyond the coastal reefs answered the question.

From 1942 to 1944, German U-boat attacks took a ghastly toll on American shipping. In spite of the vigilance of the Coast Guard and the U. S. Navy, the submarines dared to come ever closer to the shore. Any explosion confirmed the deadly cat-and-mouse game was afoot, either a U-boat striking a freighter, or our ships of war sending a German sub to a watery grave. Residents watched for the tell-tale oil and bits of wreckage on the sand. Sometimes they could guess if it was American or German, sometimes they had to wait for the rumors. And sometimes the bodies left no doubt.

No one needed to read a list of statistics or listen to speeches. Everyone knew the war was real, and very close.

Persistent rumors went around that the submarines were coming in near Little River and Murrells Inlet. The question was, could Hitler's Nazis on board the U-boats secure supplies from someone willing to do such a dastardly deed? People had helped pirates in days past; would they help the Germans? The question was asked over and over, but never satisfactorily answered.

Any stranger near the beach was closely watched. The few German immigrants were viewed with suspicion, even those who had been in this country for decades. This was one of the unfortunate aspects of both World Wars, the indiscriminate labeling of "enemy aliens" in the United States.

Almost every family had a man in the armed forces, either a husband, father, brother, cousin, or boy friend. The same groups met at the post office every day to wait for the incoming mail, or to send off cheerful, hopeful, loving letters. "V-mail," the little photographed letters written on special forms and sent quickly by air mail, became commonplace as more soldiers went overseas.

In his hometown and to his family, each serviceman wore a special aura, a touch of glamour never before known. If still stationed in the United States, he was receiving special training, or doing such an important job that he could not be spared to go overseas. If he was in the Pacific, or North Africa, or England, his folks wore a mask of gentle pride to hide the fear in their hearts.

Radios and newspapers were the only source of information. The names of news commentators became household words, as well as heads of governments, generals, and other leaders.

Anyone who heard the words, "This–is London," set against a background of gunfire and sirens, never forgot. Edward R. Murrow used this line when he opened his reports during the Battle of Britain.

New words quickly joined our vocabulary, like Blitzkrieg, Luftwaffe, Ersatz, Fifth Column, black market, buzz bombs, and concentration camps. Listening to a news report each day was like a world geography lesson, a quick study of locations and strange pronunciations.

An age of innocence still persisted in a faltering world. The good guys wore white and always overcame the bad guys, who dressed in black. If anyone doubted that important fact, they just had to go see a cowboy movie. Everyone knew the Allies would win the war–they were the good guys. It would take a little time, but the outcome was certain.

The world had been watching and waiting for so long, expecting the invasion of Hitler's "Fortress Europe," but not knowing when or where it would begin. The greatest armada of all time had assembled in southern England. More than two million troops worked and trained for long months.

Then came June 6, 1944.

The mighty attack began in the stormy pre-dawn hours of that day. Surely this was the final phase of World War II in Europe.

Americans awoke that morning to the frantic radio broadcasts of news reporters trying to keep up with fast breaking events, all within the bounds of strict censorship. The Allies had landed on Normandy and invaded France. It was D-Day.

Radio newscasters talked about Omaha and Utah beach, Cherbourg, Calais, and LeHavre. People practiced their French and waited for news of their loved ones.

Too often the news came in a dreaded telegram from the War Department. Men from Horry County were wounded or killed in the invasion and in the hard fighting that followed. The list of casualties grew at a terrible rate.

Hospitals in England filled with wounded GIs. The fighting raged deeper into France, while more and more Americans were landing there. Family members often opened precious letters from their young men to find words or sentences blacked out. People desperately wanted to know where their loved ones were, but accepted censorship as one of the costs of winning the war. Maybe it would somehow help their son or husband to stay alive.

Several Myrtle Beach men, involved in the D-Day invasion, went ashore on Utah Beach. One of them said he quickly realized if he could cross the open beach and make it to the hedgerows, he just might survive. He did. He observed that in combat a soldier better learn survival skills in a hurry. And the longer you survived, the better your chances were. He went through bitter fighting in France and Germany, and survived to return home.

Two brothers shared an unforgettable experience. The older one was wounded in Normandy on D-Day plus seven, and taken back to England. The younger one, who had just reached England, learned from family letters that his brother was in a hospital, though they didn't know where and weren't sure how bad his wounds were. After a tireless search, he located his brother in an emergency hospital in Newton Abbott, near Torquay on the southwestern coast of England. The two brothers shared a warm reunion. Both fought later in France.

One young man's family received a telegram in December, 1944, which said that he had been killed in the Battle of the Bulge, as it was later called. Again came new words: St. Lo, Liege, Bastogne, and the Bridge of Remagen. Furious deadly fighting continued on into the Rhineland.

Some Americans captured in the invasion or aftermath suffered ghastly treatment at the hands of the desperate Germans. They reported being kept in cattle cars, shuttled across the country, and sent on "death marches" through the snow with no food.

And then it was over. The war in Europe ended in total defeat for Germany on May 8, 1945.

There was little chance for celebration before the awful truths began to surface. How could average stay-at-home Americans not have known about the evils unleashed on the world by the Nazis? War crimes too terrible to comprehend included the herding of innocent people into concentration camps, gas chambers for mindless executions, and planned genocide for the Jews.

With the end of the war in Europe, many GIs went directly to the Pacific war zones. The use against Japan of a new and more horrible weapon, the atomic bomb, abruptly ended the war in the Pacific. That surrender came in September of 1945. Once again the world learned of atrocities in the treatment of native populations and war prisoners.

Soldiers began to come home. Some lay wounded in hospitals, praying to return home as soon as possible. Too many others would never come home. Horry County was sparsely settled in 1945, yet the Horry County Veterans Affairs office lists an unofficial count of deaths in battle: Navy–13, Armed Forces–76.

The war was over, but the age of innocence had ended.

The Nazi Swastika

30

The German POW Camp

From Bavaria and Hesse, the Ruhr Valley and the Rhineland, Westphalia and Saxony, they came. They were the pride of the Afrika Korps: fliers, paratroopers, infantrymen, and black-uniformed veterans of Panzer divisions. They were all deeply burned by the African sun when they came to Myrtle Beach in 1944.

These were German prisoners of war.

By the end of World War II, there were about 375,000 German prisoners of war in 511 camps in the United States. The National Works Program was activated in 1943, permitting the use of prisoners as laborers on farms, in pulpwood industries, and in reforestation programs. In 1944 America could use them. The labor force had been drained to fill the ranks of the armed forces. None of the other Allies could take care of the increasing number of German prisoners, so they came to the United States.

The American public was understandably anti-Nazi and viewed the arrival of the POWs with suspicion and apprehension. Grim pictures and stories of Nazi atrocities, as well as letters from servicemen, colored the attitudes of local residents. Years of personal suffering and sacrifice left little compassion for the ones they blamed for their problems.

German prisoners came from North Africa on the same troop carriers that transported American soldiers. As the Germans surrendered in greater numbers, more ships were needed. When Prime Minister Winston Churchill came to Washington for strategy conferences with President Roosevelt, he traveled on a ship with thousands of prisoners.

On board ship the POWs received treatment for wounds or illnesses. They ate the same food as the American GIs. As they traveled by train across the United States, they looked in vain for the toppled skyscrapers, the bombed-out cities, and the devastated countryside reported by German propaganda. The treatment of the prisoners lessened their anti-American feelings. Stripped of their proud uniforms and medals, and dressed in the drab POW garb, Prussian arrogance diminished. The prisoners became more cooperative.

In 1944 eight thousand POWs were sent to twenty camps in South Carolina. They were under the supervision of Lieutenant Colonel Wyndham M. Manning of Columbia.

Requests for workers in the Pee Dee area brought the Germans to Florence and Myrtle Beach. They were housed at Florence Army Air Field until temporary camps could be erected and labor quotas processed for nearby counties.

In Myrtle Beach army personnel hastily constructed a small camp on the north end of town, located between 71st and 79th Avenues North. A fence and guards surrounded the camp. Few civilians visited. Later the POWs were housed in barracks on Myrtle Beach Army Air Base, which they helped build. The temporary camp was totally dismantled.

There was the ever present fear that prisoners would escape. Local people heard, "Lock your doors and windows. Don't leave clothes on the lines at night. If a prisoner escapes, he will try to get civilian clothes." One lady said when her husband's old lazy dogs barked at night, she always thought a prisoner must be outside.

Some of the prisoners had grown up as "Hitler Youth." They boasted to the guards that Germany's secret weapon, the buzz bomb, would win the war. Other prisoners wept over what was happening to their country.

Two Horry County companies used about 250 POWs to cut pulpwood. Carried to the work area on trucks, the prisoners received careful instructions in the use of saws and other tools. The daily task of each prisoner was to cut one cord of wood, a job that could be done in a few hours.

Once the POWs went on strike and refused to get on the trucks. Captain James Bell secured the camp and withheld the food. When the prisoners got hungry they went back to work. No other episodes occurred.

One company used prisoners to cut pulpwood in the Bucksport vicinity. When the trucks rolled into Bucksport, the prisoners found a deserted village. The local people were afraid of them.

The guards often talked to prisoners who spoke English. One day a guard asked if the Germans knew how to "goose-step." A prisoner said they did. After the completion of work that day, the group suddenly stood up. Each man had cut a short length of tree limb for a "gun." With erect bearing and military precision, with their officer barking commands in German, the POWs goose-stepped down a narrow dirt road in the woods at Socastee.

When an army bomber crashed near a pulpwood camp, POWs pulled the pilot from the plane. They put two injured crew members on the prison truck and sent them back to the base hospital. Military police arrived at the crash site later and found the prisoners guarding the damaged plane.

Myrtle Beach Farms and Trask Farms used some of the POWs,

as did local farmers. The Germans knew nothing about the cultivation of tobacco, but they quickly learned. The men often volunteered to tinker with machinery or help with the repair or construction of farm buildings. Sometimes they ate their midday meal with the farm family, and were introduced to Southern cooking.

The prisoners earned $2.50 a day in canteen coupons for their work. The coupons could be exchanged for cigarettes, beer, candy, ice cream, or other extras. They could also purchase materials for arts and crafts. Some of the men enjoyed whittling and carving, making models of castles. Some painted remembered scenes of their homeland. A local guard said that one of the prisoners painted small portraits of his two children from snapshots.

A Murrells Inlet restaurant owner said it was his job as a teenager to drive a pickup truck to the camp, take six prisoners to the army base to work, and drive them back to the camp in the late afternoon. He found the Germans friendly and willing to work. One of them, Helmut, had been a teacher in Germany. He loved wood-carving, and made a beautiful letter opener as a gift for the young driver.

The scarcity of interpreters made dealing with the prisoners difficult, although a few of them spoke a little English. A local civil engineer who spoke fluent German remembered that the men were happy to hear "Guten Morgen" or any phrase spoken in their language. Dual language booklets began to appear in POW canteens in 1944, and English courses were offered. As the POWs learned English, they were encouraged to read travelogues and other materials about the United States.

Captain Graham Hunsucker, a West Point graduate, was one of the commanders of the prison camp. He and his wife had rooms in town at the Blue Sea Inn. On Mrs. Hunsucker's birthday, the prisoners made an unusual cake for her. It was a large pound cake, topped with candied fruits, raisins, nuts, and covered with a sugary sauce.

People driving along the King's Highway, which ran close beside the army base, could sometimes hear strains of music. On Sunday nights and special occasions the prisoners would sing marching songs, folk tunes, and carols. Their nostalgia and yearning for the homeland could only be expressed in song. Often people parked their cars along the road and sat on the grass to listen. Sometimes they brought cookies for the guards to give to the POWs.

Fritz Gorman, according to a guard who remembered him, was a model prisoner. Gorman was one of the first to be repatriated when the war ended. His home was in East Germany, and he was deeply concerned about the fate of his family as the Russians advanced. He had grown up in a twenty-five-room house on a forty-acre farm, which had belonged to his family for generations. Their main crop was sugar beets. Over and over he showed pictures of his family and expressed his fears.

One morning Deputy Sheriff Morgan "Shrimp" Lewis, driving from Windy Hill Beach to the courthouse in Conway, picked up a young man along the road. Deputy Lewis noticed the man's blond hair, good looks, and quiet demeanor. In Conway the hitchhiker indicated he wanted to get out at the clock in front of city hall. The deputy dropped off his rider, continued on, and found an uproar at the courthouse. A POW had escaped and the sheriff was organizing a search party.

Deputy Lewis, with a red face, offered to go get the prisoner. "He rode to Conway with me, and I just let him off at the clock." The deputy helped return the POW to the camp.

The prisoners were allowed to keep the uniforms in which they had been captured. One day a prisoner wore his uniform under his

POW suit to the pulpwood camp. Later in the day he slipped off to Conway. He hid the POW uniform under the Waccamaw River bridge. He made friends with two young men, and together they thumbed a ride to Myrtle Beach. After enjoying the beach and sunshine for a while, the three went to a bowling alley. There the POW was picked up by MPs, not because of his German uniform, but because he wasn't wearing a tie.

In October, 1945 the Great Pee Dee River flooded, and nearly one hundred bridges washed out. The German POWs from Florence and Myrtle Beach joined other workers to rebuild the roads and bridges.

Two deaths occurred among the prisoners. One young man drowned while swimming with a group in the ocean off Myrtle Beach State Park. He was buried in Ocean Woods Memorial Cemetery. Another POW, depressed and unable to face an uncertain future, committed suicide on V-E Day when he learned of Germany's total defeat. He had worked as an orderly in the base hospital.

On V-E Day, many of the prisoners had already gone out to work when the news came. The guards loaded the men on the trucks and took them back to camp, where the announcement was read to them. They were heartsick. Some of the "Nazi Youth" had continued to think the news they heard in camp was only American propaganda. They felt certain Germany was really winning the war. But all of them worried about their loved ones at home.

The war had ended, but some prisoners were reluctant to leave. They had been well-fed and well-treated, and they had experienced a different way of life. No violations of the Geneva Convention were reported in the prison camps in South Carolina. By the end of 1946, all of the prisoners had left the camps for staging areas and repatriation.

There are records of about five hundred POWs, men who had been in prison camps across the United States, who returned later to become American citizens.

31

America's Most Beautiful Old Band Organ

Its music is probably unlike any other you've ever heard; the sound is loud and harsh. How else could it be heard over the competing noises of the amusement park at the Myrtle Beach Pavilion?

The massive old band organ, built a century ago, continues to fascinate vacationers year after year with the exact beat of its music and the sight of its dancing hand-carved figures. Children love it.

The organ was built at Walkirch in Baden, Germany in the late 1890s by A. Ruth & Sohn. Skilled craftsmen carved the figures and decorations from the finest woods, and painstakingly painted and lacquered them. The organ was specifically designed and built for the World Exposition in Paris in 1900. Hundreds of thousands of people from all over the world attended the Exposition and viewed the exhibits, which included the Eiffel Tower. The organ was a popular featured attraction in the year-long event.

Following the Exposition, the German government took the organ back home and used it to entertain its music loving population. A large wagon, pulled by a team of six horses, moved the organ from town to town so it could be seen and enjoyed by more people.

In the 1920s, after World War I, the organ became the property of a wealthy American industrialist who had heard about it during the war. He brought it to America and placed it in a specially built room in his home on Martha's Vineyard, Massachusetts. There it played for his family, friends, and visiting musicians for thirty years. Its fame spread.

In the 1950s Myrtle Beach Farms Company began to improve and expand the pavilion's amusement park. Mr. Harry Beach went to Martha's Vineyard to view the famous organ, and see if he could buy it for the company. His mission was successful. In 1954 the organ was shipped to Myrtle Beach. The amusement park has been its home ever since.

The organ stands eleven feet high, seven feet deep, and twenty feet long. It weighs about two tons. It has four hundred pipes, ninety-eight keys, and eighteen realistic hand-carved figures. Twelve of the figures move in a set rhythm with the music. They dance, play the drums, or pluck harp strings.

The player mechanism uses folding sheets of perforated cardboard. One mile of music cards came with the organ to Myrtle Beach. Much of the music is badly worn, but the program offered is still varied and enjoyable. Card No. 5 is entirely American compositions, but most of the other music is by German composers.

The unusual old organ sits at the amusement park in the midst of the rides. It is securely encased in a wooden structure that has protected it through two major hurricanes, numerous winter storms and rainy seasons, and years of heat and variable weather. Year-round high tides, nearby pounding surf, and salt-spray-laden winds attack buildings and equipment farther inland, but the organ stands secure and unharmed in its protective shelter.

During the beach season, the organ's evening concert begins at eight o'clock. Long before that time the benches in front of the organ are filled, with many people standing and waiting. Baby strollers are parked close by so small children can see and hear.

The old organ still attracts a crowd to hear its exact rhythm

Suddenly the lights go on, the wooden doors fold back, and the first chords of music swell over and above the amusement park sounds. Children and adults sit awe-struck if they are watching for the first time. The simple pattern of movements, the staccato precision of rhythm, and the classical or semi-classical music appeal to our sense of order and dignity.

The children wonder, "How can the organ play by itself?"

The pipes use compressed air, originally powered by a hand-operated wheel. An electric motor now supplies the energy.

In a day of movies, videos, computers, and live entertainment of all kinds, the simplicity of the old band organ still attracts viewers whenever it plays. Perhaps it is a symbol of an earlier day, a day when simple pleasures were cherished.

32

The Carousel

The beautiful carousel in the Myrtle Beach Pavilion Amusement Park is one of the oldest and finest in the country. Herschell-Spillman Company of New York City built the fifty-figure masterpiece in the early 1900s. The craftsmen completed most of the figures about 1912, but two elephants date back to 1890. The company built five hand-carved and custom finished carousels at the same time. The one in Myrtle Beach is the only one still in use.

A single wooden horse from these old carousels may sell for as much as thirty thousand dollars. They stay in constant demand as original folk art. The newer metal and plastic figures are not as valuable. Small porcelain copies of the horses have also become collectors' items. The late Earl Husted, vice-president and general manager of the pavilion, said in an interview some years ago that he valued the carousel at one million dollars, but even at that it could never be replaced.

The Oxford Lake Park in Anniston, Alabama first owned the carousel. In 1950 the Myrtle Beach Farms Company enlarged and beautified the pavilion's amusement park, and bought the carousel to replace a smaller merry-go-round. When it was installed, an electric Wurlitzer organ replaced the original calliope.

Fairs and amusement parks have attracted children of all ages for

The beautiful old carousel, built in the
early 1900s, attracts riders of all ages

centuries. In Medieval Europe, "market day" was held regularly in little crossroads settlements. People came from all around to enjoy the games and amusements. Jugglers, magicians, circus performers, clowns, and minstrels encouraged their viewers to watch the shows and buy the goods.

The "roundabout" was a forerunner of the merry-go-round, and the name is still used in England. Small, patient donkeys, tethered to a central pole, plodded around a large circle to the delight of their young riders. Often the donkeys were decorated with ribbons, flowers, and straw hats. With the development of steam power in the 1800s, carved figures replaced the donkeys. These figures moved along a circular track, accompanied by the shrill music of the steam calliope pipes.

The name "carousel" dates back to tournament games at the court of King Henry IV of France, in the 1500s.

The first ride at the Myrtle Beach Pavilion was a small merry-go-round. Other rides were added as the park expanded. A carousel is still the traditional central ride in an amusement park.

In the spring each part of the carousel is carefully inspected, serviced, cleaned, and the paint touched up. The figures look so fresh that they often attract artists to sketch or paint their favorite. Four of the carousel horses have appeared on U. S. postage stamps.

Special hurricane doors protect the carousel and organ from drenching rains, freezing weather, and high winds. With the doors securely in place, the carousel came through Hurricane Hazel in 1954 and Hurricane Hugo in 1989 with only minor damage to the doors.

A pavilion attendant recalls hearing a lady say that her grandmother used to bring her to ride on a special horse, and now she had brought her granddaughter to ride on "her" horse.

Whatever its name, the French Carousel, the English Roundabout, the hobby horses, or the merry-go-round, the carousel attracts generation after generation of excited, smiling riders.

33

The Gray Man of Pawley's Island

In 1993 the television show *Unsolved Mysteries* told the story of the Gray Man. The show featured a Pawley's Island couple who claimed their lives and property were spared during Hurricane Hugo because of the Gray Man's warning.

The legend of the Gray Man has been around a long time. He has been seen before and during storms for more than a century and a half.

Early in September of 1822, a horse carrying a handsome young man galloped along the sandy road that led to Pawley's Island. The man had just returned from a two-year stay in Europe, where he completed his education and went on a "Grand Tour." His man-servant, who had accompanied him on the trip, rode a horse behind his master's. The young man hurried because he was going to see his lovely fiancée, who awaited him at her father's beach home. She had made preparations for his return, and had promised their wedding would take place soon.

Impatient to see his love, the young man swerved onto a side trail, thinking he was taking a short cut. Unfortunately the path led to a marshy bog. The horse stumbled and pitched its rider headfirst into the innocent looking but deadly coastal quicksand. The servant leaped from his saddle and desperately tried to help his master, but the quicksand sucked both the young man and his horse under. The servant stared at the smooth surface of the bog, hoping to see some sign of life. There was none.

Later the fiancée opened her door, thinking the knock came from her lover, but instead she found the stunned servant. When she heard what had happened, she collapsed.

For days she lay in bed alone, refusing to eat or sleep.

The young woman's parents feared for her health, and finally talked her into going for a walk on the beach. She found some comfort from her grief while strolling beside the gently-breaking waves. Her walk on the beach became a daily habit. Late one afternoon, as the evening shadows deepened and the fog drifted in, the young woman walked alone beside the ocean. In the distance she saw a man, dressed in gray, moving slowly toward her through the mist. As she drew closer she was sure it was her dead lover. She cried out and ran toward him. The man gestured toward the mainland, then vanished in the swirling mist.

The young woman returned to her beach home and went to bed. Seeing the man had left her confused and uneasy. She finally drifted off to sleep, and dreamed of a terrible storm sweeping toward the island. She told her father the next day about the Gray Man, and about her dream. Her father decided she was losing her mind, and rushed her to a doctor in Charleston.

Soon after the family left the island, the hurricane of 1822 struck. It was one of the worst storms on record, resulting in tremendous loss of life and property. Homes were wrenched from their foundations and splintered.

The father changed his mind about his daughter's madness after the storm struck. When the family returned to Pawley's Island, they felt sure they would find their home in ruins. Amazingly, it sat unharmed, surrounded by damaged and destroyed houses.

Other people said that they had seen a man in gray come ashore during the storm, then disappear.

The Gray Man has given many warnings since 1822. Residents spotted him before Hurricane Hazel in 1954, Hurricane Gracie in 1959, and Hurricane Hugo in 1989.

Today we rely on the Weather Bureau, with their computers, satellites, and advanced technology to warn us of approaching storms.

But if you see the Gray Man, take heed. He may be trying to save your life.

34

Hurricane Hugo

September 21, 1989 ranks as one of the Grand Strand's most unforgettable nights. After days of uncertainty, Hurricane Hugo zeroed in on coastal lands during the night, and then plowed inland.

The damage done by the storm was astronomical in cost, and its effect may still be seen in forested areas near the coast and farther inland. The eye of the vast storm moved ashore just north of Charleston, with islands near the city and the villages of Awendaw and McClellanville bearing the brunt of the initial thrust of winds and water.

Myrtle Beach lies at the center of the coastal curve known as Long Bay. This cove effect offers some protection. The beaches near the outer limits of Long Bay felt Hugo's wrath more strongly. Ocean Drive and Cherry Grove to the north, and Surfside, Garden City, Murrells Inlet, Huntington State Park, Pawleys Island, and Debidue Beach to the south all suffered more damage than Myrtle Beach.

Hurricane Hugo was graded a Category 4 storm, the second highest level. At the time it felt like the worst one ever to hit the Grand Strand, although Hurricane Hazel in 1954 still serves as the symbol of devastation. Some people called Hugo "Hazel's son," classing them together in intensity. With high winds, the water surge and tornadoes around the main storm are an extra source of danger. And they strike at random.

This is damage from Hurricane Hazel in 1954.
Hugo is often called "Hazel's son."
Courtesy of the Horry County Museum

On that September night, Hugo raged up and down the coast. Fishing villages were destroyed, among them the town of McClellan-ville, south of Georgetown. Boats splintered, oyster beds were wiped out, and the fishing and shrimping industry hit a standstill for months to come. The water surge moved inland with the high tide. Residents went to the old school building on Main Street, a designated storm shelter. As the water rose and swirled through the classrooms, the people moved to the second floor and stood on tables and chairs. The water kept rising, right up to the second floor. The people barely escaped with their lives. Families still at home climbed into attics. Many houses were swept off their foundations. One woman and her children survived by tying themselves to a tree.

In Myrtle Beach, the erratic winds might strike one building and leave others close by unscathed. An example of this was First United Methodist Church, located on the corner on Ninth Avenue North and the King's Highway. Established in 1919, First United was the first church in Myrtle Beach. The heavy wooden steeple, built in 1939, was picked up by the wind and dropped through the roof of the structure. It just missed the balcony as it crashed into the main part of the sanctuary, on top of collapsed and splintered pews. Heavy rain poured in through the ragged hole in the roof.

After the storm, the big church without its steeple was a landmark and topic of conversation for visitors.

The storm struck other parts of Myrtle Beach hard with high tides and lashing winds. Still, the storm's intensity was less than at other places. Hugo pounded its way across the coast and then hundreds of miles inland. People found themselves without power or fresh water for days or weeks.

Amid the debris and destruction of the storm, clearing and rebuilding began immediately. Work crews went out daily from churches and agencies in Myrtle Beach to help beaches and villages that were in even greater need. Optimism prevailed in the minds of residents, with emphasis on helping. Most people had experienced other storms over the years. The unstated philosophy was that if you chose to live at the beach, along with the beauty and normally pleasant climate, you should expect storms.

In the 1950s, tremendous growth and development took place following Hurricane Hazel. The destruction caused by Hugo gave new impetus, once again, to rebuilding and expanding on an even greater scale. Myrtle Beach and the entire Grand Strand are rising from the ashes of wreckage, and blossoming anew.

Blanche W. Floyd was born in Marion, South Carolina and grew up in the Low Country. She has lived in Myrtle Beach since 1950 with her husband, J. K. Floyd. They have three children. Blanche received her Bachelor's Degree from Columbia College, and a Master's Degree from the University of South Carolina. She taught history in Myrtle Beach schools until 1980. She has had over one hundred articles published in newspapers and magazines. *Tales along the Grand Strand of South Carolina* is her third book.